"Just as graduation is called a commencement and not a termination, one's life is about the never-ending beginnings we all experience through loss and change. The courageous recreate themselves and their lives and enter love's service because of their wounds. Read and learn from Judy's experience."

—Bernie Siegel, MD,
author of *365 Prescriptions for the Soul*
and *Prescriptions for Living*

"From loss to renewal, *STUNNED by Grief* provides clear, inspirational steps to manage the death of a loved one. There isn't a single solution, or prescription; rather, a series of personal thoughts and actions derived from Brizendine's own experience and those of others. Everyone, from military spouse to parents and friends, will find calm, steady guidance that resonates. Definitely a book worth reading, as we all need inspiration to overcome our personal loss, and reminders of the joy of life and the strength of the human spirit."

—Scott Rutter (LTC, U.S. Army, Ret.),
national spokesman, Tragedy Assistance
Program for Survivors (TAPS)

"*STUNNED by Grief* brings purpose and direction to the painful grief process from someone who's been there. Judy shares 'real life' as she reveals how God can give you strength and courage to overcome tragedy. *STUNNED* will meet you right where you are. It's a book about grief unlike any other."

—Darrell and Stevie Waltrip,
founders of Motor Racing Outreach
FOX Sports commentator and
former NASCAR Winston Cup champion

"This book is a true gem and a must read for anyone who has experienced the grief of a close personal loss. The author opens her heart, mind, and, most importantly, her soul to examine the devastation of her husband's death and her ultimate triumph through her faith in God. This book is a true inspiration. She is painfully honest, open, and extremely uplifting in her writing."

—Gary L. Malone, MD,
board certified psychiatrist and psychoanalyst
author of *Five Keys for Understanding Men: A Woman's Guide*

"Ready or not—the experience of the death of a loved one is stunning. Like being left blindfolded in a deep dark jungle, finding one's way to a safe and familiar territory will overwhelm you with hopelessness. You might ask, 'If only someone who has been here could walk me through this . . .?' Well, your map and guide are within your grasp.

"More than just answers, Judy Brizendine will 'red dot' your heart's location and give you a clear sense of direction and renewed destiny. My wife Jeannie and I serve as pastors to Judy. She is a joy to work closely and passionately with, and we love doing 'life' with her and Jon. We both trust Judy, and the God she has come to know in a deeper way through her pain. Pain that can now become your gain. You will laugh, live, and yes, love again!"

—Phil Munsey,
founding pastor, Life Church
author of *Legacy Now: Why Everything about You Matters*

"Out of her tears and personal grief, Judy Brizendine has created a warm and sensitive message that is filled with great wisdom, practical help—and a pathway of hope for the future. Make this book a gift to every person you know who is in the midst of grief."

—Paul A. Eshleman,
vice president, Campus Crusade for Christ, International

"Judy has so eloquently portrayed the process of grieving and of subsequent healing. Reading her excellent book has released a river of Hope that springs eternal. I am amazed at the insights and clarity that she projects. Many will be blessed who read it."

—Moses and Betty Vegh,
Ambassadors of Hope to the Nations

"For anyone who has ever walked through the dark days of grief—or knows someone who is there right now—*STUNNED by Grief* is a must. You'll find hope, help, and honesty between these pages. Written by one who has been there, *STUNNED* will encourage and equip those caught in the throes of loss."

—J.P. Jones,
senior pastor, Crossline Community Church

—Donna Jones,
speaker and author

Also available from this author

STUNNED *by Grief Journal*

STUNNED
BY GRIEF

REMAPPING YOUR LIFE
WHEN LOSS CHANGES EVERYTHING

Judy Brizendine

BennettKnepp
PUBLISHING

Lake Forest, CA

STUNNED by Grief: Remapping Your Life When Loss Changes Everything
Copyright © 2011 by Judy Luttrell Brizendine
Published by BennettKnepp Publishing

Printed in the United States of America

Scripture quotations marked (*NIV*) are taken from the *HOLY BIBLE, NEW INTERNATIONAL VERSION*®. *NIV*®. Copyright © 1973, 1978, 1984 by International Bible Society. Used by permission of Zondervan. All rights reserved. Scripture quotations marked (*MSG*) are taken from *THE MESSAGE*. Copyright © by Eugene H. Peterson 1993, 1994, 1995, 1996, 2000, 2001, 2002. Used by permission of NavPress Publishing Group. All rights reserved. Scripture quotations marked (*NLT*) are taken from the *Holy Bible, New Living Translation*, Copyright © 1996. Used by permission of Tyndale House Publishers, Inc., Wheaton, Illinois 60189. All rights reserved. Scripture quotations marked (*God's Word*) are taken from the *GOD'S WORD*® *Translation*. Copyright © 1995 by God's Word to the Nations. Used by permission. All rights reserved. Scripture quotations marked (*TLB*) are taken from *The Living Bible*. Copyright © 1971 by Tyndale House Publishers, Inc., Wheaton, Illinois 60189. All rights reserved. Scripture quotations marked (*NKJV*) are taken from the *New King James Version*®. Copyright © 1982 by Thomas Nelson, Inc. Used by permission. All rights reserved. Scripture quotations marked (*Good News Bible: TEV*) are taken from the *Good News Translation— Second Edition*. Copyright © 1992 by American Bible Society. Used by permission. Scripture quotations marked (*AMP*) are taken from *THE AMPLIFIED BIBLE*®, Copyright © 1954, 1958, 1962, 1964, 1965, 1987 by The Lockman Foundation. All rights reserved. Used by permission. (www.Lockman.org).

Reprinted by permission. "*The Great House of God*, Max Lucado, © 1997, Thomas Nelson Inc. Nashville, Tennessee. All rights reserved." Reprinted by permission. "*Healing Is a Choice*, Stephen Arterburn, © 2005, Thomas Nelson Inc. Nashville, Tennessee. All rights reserved." From: *Life Is Goodbye/Life Is Hello: Grieving Well Through All Kinds of Loss* by Alla Renée Bozarth, Ph.D. Copyright © 1994 by HAZELDEN FOUNDATION. Reprinted by permission of Hazelden Foundation, Center City, MN.

Extension of Copyright Page appears on page 257

DISCLAIMER: Please read page 259.

Publisher's Cataloging-in-Publication Data (Prepared by The Donohue Group, Inc.)
Brizendine, Judy.
    Stunned by grief : remapping your life when loss changes everything / Judy Brizendine.
    p. : ill. ; cm.
    Includes bibliographical references and index.
    ISBN: 978-0-9831688-1-2 (paperback)
    ISBN: 978-0-9831688-2-9 (ePDF)
    ISBN: 978-0-9831688-3-6 (ePUB)
    ISBN: 978-0-9831688-4-3 (Kindle/Mobi)
    1. Grief--Religious aspects. 2. Grief--Psychological aspects. 3. Bereavement--Religious aspects. 4. Bereavement--Psychological aspects. 3. Loss (Psychology) 4. Adjustment (Psychology) 5. Spiritual healing. I. Title.

BV4905.3 .B75 2011
248.8/6/6   2010917535

Credits: Cover and interior design by DesignForBooks.com. Cover photos: Author photo, Jon Kreider © 2011; clouds, iStockphoto © dusipuffi; silhouette image, open source art by Lu Feng. Editor: Susan Malone, Malone Editorial Services.

DEDICATION

. . . first and foremost, I dedicate this book to God.

Without His love, inspiration, presence, and hope, I would not be telling my story.

. . . to each person who shared your journey with us by participating in the grief-support workshops Jon and I facilitated.

I extend my deepest thanks. We received far more from each of you than can possibly be imagined—and more than we could ever give back. Priceless insights came directly from you, and your words and experiences interwoven throughout this book will inform, comfort, encourage, strengthen, and give hope to others facing the pain of grief.

. . . to my dear husband and best friend, Jon Kreider, my partner in every area of life, including our mutual desire to convey God's love to grieving people.

Your passion about helping others face grief inspired me to give more of myself, and convinced me that I have a meaningful story to share. Only a strong, secure man could handle reading entries from his wife's journal about her late husband, even if a worthwhile purpose is involved. Seeing the words in print for everyone else to read is even more difficult. However, you firmly agreed that we can help people in a more powerful way by being transparent about grief, and your commitment took precedence over any personal discomfort.

I am very happy God's plan for my future included such a caring, generous, and wonderful man. And I'm grateful that we've been given a second chance for love after losing both of our spouses to death.

. . . to the precious life and memory of my late husband, John Brizendine.

Your death began my struggle with grief, but the sorrow evolved into a slowly unfolding story of hope. This book is a way of honoring your memory and bringing something good out of the most painful period of my life. If the truth about my experience helps anyone, then telling it is worthwhile. That's what the circle of life is all about, isn't it—each of us loving and helping one another.

———

Celebrating the lives of:
John A. Brizendine III (Maj., USMC, Ret.), my husband
William L. Luttrell, my dad
Verlene Kreider, Jon's mom
Donna Kreider, Jon's wife

———

CONTENTS

Part Two—Remapping My Life
Where Do I Go from Here?

Part Three—Interactive Exercises
Remapping Tools

Part Four—Hope
You Still Have a Future

PREFACE

Do what you can with what you have, right where you are.

—THEODORE ROOSEVELT

Why write a book about grief? Because, frankly, when the harsh reality of my husband's death became real, I had absolutely *no idea* what to do. I was painfully unprepared to face grief and the effects of loss. And the thought of others (just like me) struggling to gain control over something they can't grasp or explain, concerns me deeply.

Grief is not what we expect, and its reality is nothing we can imagine.

Grievers urgently need to know what is happening. But pain alters one's ability to focus. I understand. Steady concentration was a battle for me, and a regular complaint among grief-group members. Despite the difficulty, you need information. Because of my challenging experience, I want to ease the way for other hurting people to navigate through the fear, confusion, and uncertainty of their grief journeys without bogging down in too many details—or groping to find answers.

This book is different. Think of it as a no-nonsense look at the essentials. When you read this material, you will readily understand the basics—what you really need to know at first about grief. You will find out about critical obstacles and challenges—*flashpoints*—to expect during your grief. And you'll learn about what is happening and what to do.

Rather than a comprehensive look at the subject by a therapist or medical professional, this book is a fellow traveler's down-to-earth approach to grief. It breaks down the material into bite-sized pieces that are easy to follow for anyone going through the distress of grief. You do not have to read the book straight through; in fact, if you quickly need help with a certain topic, turn to any chapter or section and read it separately.

Grief is not what we expect, and its reality is nothing we can imagine.

I am an ongoing survivor of grief and this book is the story of my journey—that of a person who faced devastating loss firsthand and slowly worked through it. It's a book about insight. And change. The details are intimate. By revealing an inside look at grief, my aim is to give a realistic perspective. I want you to know what to expect.

Also, I have connected with others who are experiencing the effects of pain and loss by facilitating grief-support groups. During these workshops, certain key issues repeatedly surfaced—either because they were especially hard to handle (complex, explosive, or unpredictable), or because they were essential in a participant's journey toward healing. This book accentuates these crucial topics.

Grief, hope, determination, and faith are the focus of this easy-to-read guide meant to inform, inspire, encourage, and support all those facing the loss of someone vitally important. While my perspective is that of a person who lost her husband unexpectedly, this book presents relevant information to anyone facing profound loss and trying to understand it.

My goal throughout the book is to come alongside you—wherever you are—and help you unscramble the turmoil of grief. My desire is to comfort you as you face your own grief questions and uncertainties. I will tell you about things I wish I had known. I want to encourage you with hope, and convince you that you *do* still have a future—and that your future can be positive and meaningful.

> Grief is a demanding, confusing detour in life's journey, but it is not the final destination. Your road does not end here.

I wish you Godspeed as you travel toward healing.

You are not alone. God loves you more than you can possibly imagine. And He's looking for you, even if you're not yet trying to find Him.

Judy Brizendine

Judy Brizendine

P.S. At the end of each chapter is a "Thought to Write About." These statements and questions provide an opportunity for you to write your thoughts and feelings about the subject covered in the chapter.

Just start writing . . . about what is tearing at your heart, what you can't stop thinking about, what keeps you awake at night, makes you angry, frightens you, confuses you, what you're grateful for, or whatever comes into your mind.

Writing—or journaling—helps release everything bottled up tightly inside. Sometimes talking about personal feelings is difficult, so writing helps you process these painful emotions and advances your healing.

Pick up a journal or notebook and start writing.

You have nothing to lose and everything to gain.

The best way out is always through.

—Robert Frost

ACKNOWLEDGMENTS

(and my heartfelt thanks)

. . . to Nancy Wilder, for your painstaking manuscript review (twice) and deeply insightful recommendations and comments. A keen understanding of grief based on your own painful journey, a deep, abiding spiritual relationship, and your commanding skill created a priceless editorial combination.

. . . to Becky McPheron, for your capable, thorough manuscript review (twice, also) as a professional who has spent a lifetime pursuing a passion for the written word. Thanks, too, for your perspective and suggestions, as my cherished friend of thirty-plus years and someone who has also experienced grief.

. . . to Kathy Jo Stones, a licensed therapist with a passion for helping those suffering from grief, for wisdom and suggestions from your unique viewpoint and experience, as well as your encouragement and prayers at the very beginning of the process.

. . . to my daughter, Kelly D'Innocenti, for your pointed questions and valued opinions as you read through the early stages of the book, as well as your love, respect, and ever-present loyalty and support. You *always* make me smile.

. . . to my mom, Wilda Luttrell, for your helpful suggestions, comments, and patience in wading through the earliest version of the book, and for your constant love and prayers. Everyone who knows you, loves you—and why not?

. . . to Debbie Mullen, for your honest feedback as a fellow grief traveler on the journey toward healing, and for your willingness to be available to help other people on the same path. You are an inspiration.

. . . to Marie Grosshuesch, for your enthusiastic encouragement, advice, and moral support; for your willingness to recommend trusted resources; and for your constant readiness to help.

. . . to Karen Witzke, for graciously reviewing a list of subtitle options (from someone you didn't even know!) and then crafting an ideal combination that perfectly expressed the message.

. . . to my editor, Susan Malone, for your matchless editorial review and analysis of my manuscript. You are a genius! A pointed question here, a comment there—and you *coaxed* me into infusing more life (and sharing more of myself) into the book, giving people real tools and concrete hope to sink their teeth into. When I thought I *was* showing "how to," you made me realize I needed to say more. Thanks for teaching me to think in another way. Working with you was pure pleasure.

. . . to Susan Kendrick and Graham Van Dixhorn (Write to Your Market), for your skill (and art) in drilling down to key words and concepts that powerfully *capture* and convey a message. The effect is compelling. Your recommendations were more valuable than you'll ever know.

. . . to Michael Rohani, my designer, for persevering to come up with an out-of-the-box concept that expresses the book's message in a sensitive, hopeful and innovative way. A creative and consummate professional, you really listened and met the challenge head-on! Thank you!

. . . to my exceptional husband, Jon Kreider, for your advice and criticism, unwavering support and encouragement, and untold sacrifice through this long, rewarding process. You've been my biggest cheerleader—and most enthusiastic promoter! You postponed your own wishes, willingly accepted the financial impact, and supported the many hours I sat in front of my computer refining words and ideas (and never stopped believing in, and affirming our shared dream to change the way the world views grief), to help people find their way through one of the toughest experiences in life. My love, gratitude, and respect go to you, now and always.

. . . and to everyone who participated, encouraged, listened, prayed, made recommendations, or was in any way connected . . . saying 'thank you' doesn't seem adequate, but know that it comes from the bottom of my heart! Mentioning everyone who played a part in the process is impossible, but each person's involvement was undeniably important. I couldn't have done it without you.

PART
ONE

UNPACKING GRIEF

What Is Happening to Me?

INTRODUCTION

Life changes fast . . . Life changes in the instant.
The ordinary instant.

—JOAN DIDION
(FROM *The Year of Magical Thinking*)

You're probably wondering what happened to bring me to this place, so I'll briefly share my story with you. Little did I know my life was about to change—irreversibly and *forever*. While that statement may sound dramatic, if you are reading this book, in all likelihood either you or someone you love has experienced grief. Tragedy generally strikes unexpectedly, while we are just living our everyday lives.

On a beautiful spring morning in April 1998, everything was terrific. I was content. My marriage was happier than it had ever been, and I was working in a challenging, satisfying design career.

When we moved to southern California several years earlier, we did not know anyone so we had to start at square one. Establishing ties and settling into our new community took time and effort, but now we were comfortably entrenched in a routine and lifestyle. We had joined a dynamic church, formed close friendships, and discovered many ways to enjoy our new surroundings.

At last, all seemed to be in order. Such was life on Saturday morning, April 25. I had absolutely no idea, vague uneasiness, or any sort of premonition that at exactly 2:44 P.M. that afternoon, in a split second my entire life would change.

My life mate, best friend, and constant companion of nearly thirty years, my husband John went on a mountain bike ride, as he had done hundreds of times before. I kissed him good-bye as he finished preparing for his ride. The next time I saw John was a day later—at the mortuary—to identify his autopsied body. Details of that thirty-something-hour interval and its harsh reality are permanently engraved in my mind.

After completing my errands, I returned home late in the afternoon. John should have been back from his bike ride, as we had planned to meet friends at church. At first, I was not concerned, simply thinking he had taken a longer ride. However, as the time continued to pass, fear crept in. My husband was overly reliable, and his failure to show up on time was uncharacteristic.

I didn't know what to do. John had gone on a mountain bike ride—so he could have been anywhere. I did not actually know where to look. But I had to do *something*. I started driving down roads he might have traveled on his way to the "off-road" locations, hoping to spot him in case he had run into trouble on his way home. This search was futile, so I returned home. Two friends met me there.

Unsettled, dazed, scared, I did not know what to think. A sense of foreboding settled over me like heavy fog. My stomach churned.

Something terrible had happened—I just had no idea what it was. I called several hospital emergency rooms, but found no answers. Images and questions frantically darted through my mind. Was John injured and lying somewhere on the side of the mountain? Had he been involved in an accident on the road? Had an animal attacked him? He had encountered mountain lions on previous rides.

Several hours had passed beyond the time I expected John to be home. I called the office of the Orange County Sheriff to inquire about my husband and request help.

Soon after my phone call, a sheriff's deputy arrived. He opened his laptop computer and began to ask all sorts of questions as he filled out his report. The detailed inquiry seemed to drag on forever. Periodically, the deputy made and received phone calls. I did not realize he was painstakingly trying to piece together all the parts of the gradually unfolding puzzle.

For some unknown reason, on this particular day, John was riding without any identification. I had no way of knowing that emergency room personnel had already pronounced him dead (at 2:44 in the afternoon) as an unidentified "John Doe." Many hours passed before the authorities were able to process the information I supplied, along with military medical and dental records, to identify my husband's body.

John was less than a mile from home when a massive heart attack hit, accompanied by a fatal arrhythmia. He had taken a short cut through an apartment-complex parking lot, and when he collapsed, someone saw him and called 911. John was unconscious when the paramedics arrived. He never regained consciousness. The event happened without warning.

Images of that evening remain with me today. The deputy excused himself and went outside to retrieve something from his car. When he returned, two officials from the coroner's office came with him. Dispassionately, they said John was dead. They informed me that he had had a heart attack. I didn't believe their report, and told them so. The details they conveyed were sketchy, but they handed me a small bag containing a few of his personal belongings—a worn, soiled, blue nylon fanny pack, a small set of bicycle-repair tools, and a black sport wristwatch. John could not possibly be dead, so why did they have his things? Nothing made sense.

How surreal that night was. I had only heard of the term "out of body experience," but that night, I felt as though I had stepped outside of myself. Observing everything that was happening in the room, I even heard myself talk—somehow separated from my physical body. I felt as though a movie were playing before my eyes, except I was actually *in* the movie.

> *I did not make it through the toughest experience of my life on my own.*

I vividly remember phone calls to tell the unspeakable news to family and friends. The worst was a dreaded and heart-wrenching call to our daughter, Kelly. She was out of town, and I tried for hours to reach her—not to tell her the news about John, but to ask her to come directly to our house when she returned. Yet she demanded to know what was wrong. She was distraught and hysterical.

Unexpected death. Instantly, my entire world—and the way I related to it—changed. Only those who have experienced the devastating loss of someone extremely close will understand. Only those who have faced, firsthand, the unbelievable depths of grief have the *capacity* to understand. And until my grief experience, I did not understand either.

Incomprehensible, indescribable grief. Thus began an inescapable journey—one I did not expect and certainly did not want. Yet, this unwelcome journey has been a life-changing experience of widespread proportions—with changes that are still happening today, more than twelve years later.

I did not make it through the toughest experience of my life on my own. My faith in God gave me the will to go on when the pain was more than I could bear. He helped me do what I could not do alone. He did not let me down. He took care of me.

In spite of everything, I can tell you with absolute certainty there *is* hope, even during the darkest, seemingly most hopeless times of grief. I can also tell you with confidence that, in time, your life can be rich, satisfying, and fulfilling in new ways because of your grief experience—*if you allow it to be so.* The choice is yours.

> *Grief is a process.*
> *It takes time.*
> *Hold on.*

Grief is a process. It takes time. Hold on.

And remember, hope is still alive, even if you can't see it yet.

> *Just as an acorn holds the promise of a mighty, towering oak (and from a seemingly lifeless cocoon emerges an amazing, glorious butterfly), the miracle of hope lives within you . . .*

—JUDY BRIZENDINE

1

WHAT DOES GRIEF LOOK LIKE —AND HOW DOES IT PROGRESS?

*Grief comes in unexpected surges . . . mysterious cues that set
off a reminder of grief.
It comes crashing like a wave, sweeping me in its crest, twisting
me inside out.
Then recedes, leaving me broken.
Oh, Mama, I don't want to eat, to walk, to get out of bed.
Reading, working, cooking, listening, mothering.
Nothing matters.
I do not want to be distracted from my grief.
I wouldn't mind dying.
I wouldn't mind it at all.*

—TOBY TALBOT
(FROM *A Book About My Mother*)

GRIEF—in the beginning is . . .

. . . an overwhelming, indescribable pain

. . . all-consuming

. . . shocking and numbing to our senses

. . . aloneness

. . . a multitude of tangled emotions

. . . an altered reality

. . . heavy and exhausting

. . . a total upheaval

. . . an inward-focused look

GRIEF, as it progresses, is . . .

. . . a disorderly process

. . . a journey through unknown territory

. . . unpredictable tears

. . . ocean waves that crash suddenly upon us

. . . an intense emotional pain and sadness

. . . moments of sharp, unexpected anger

. . . living life on "autopilot"

. . . at times, completely draining—physically, emotionally,
      and spiritually

. . . intermingled with fear, anxiety, and confusion

. . . realization of shattered dreams

You may also experience . . .

. . . hollowness

. . . detachment, disconnection

. . . a state of lost security and instability

. . . difficulty concentrating and making decisions

. . . overly sensitive feelings

. . . physical discomfort—such as tightness in the chest; rapid heartbeat or skipped beats; sleep disruption; change in eating habits; nausea; and hyperactivity or complete exhaustion

Along with grief comes . . .

. . . the need to talk

. . . the need to be heard

. . . the need to know someone cares (really cares)

GRIEF—later on (could be years after the loss), may show up as . . .

. . . tears, especially when triggered by reminders

. . . changes in feelings, thoughts, and attitudes—"new perspectives"

. . . a changed identity and new roles

. . . an ongoing, lengthy recovery that lasts much longer than we wish or think

. . . a remapping of life—a need to form new routines, interests, and relationships

. . . a *progression* of letting go or "release"

. . . a new "normal" (whatever that is for you)

and then, *perhaps* . . .

. . . refocused thinking and planning

. . . a new examination of life, priorities, and faith

. . . a greater awareness of others' needs and hurts

. . . a heightened sense of time's finite nature

. . . renewal within yourself (if you choose)

. . . new dreams for your future

GRIEF—*possibilities*, even later in the process, may include . . .

. . . a desire to help others

. . . a compassion for others

. . . a greater comprehension of love

. . . personal growth

. . . a stronger faith and desire to know God at a deeper level

Grief—unpredictable, disorderly, disruptive, unimaginable— is difficult to capture in words, and even tougher to comprehend. Grief—a confusing maze—is as hard to navigate as to understand.

> Grief is like a foreign language when we first confront it: awkward, unfamiliar, unwieldy, and overwhelming.

Making sense of the chaos of grief is a process of your own design carried out on your timetable, along with certain people you choose to let in as you travel your path to healing.

Take one step at a time. You're stronger than you think. You *can* do this, and it's worth the price. But no one else can do it for you.

You may feel as though you are alone, but God promises He will not leave you, He is in control, and He has good plans in store for you. Trust His words. And hold on to His promises. Hold on tight.

I know what I'm doing.

I have it all planned out—plans to take care of you,

    not abandon you,

      plans to give you the future you hope for.

—Jeremiah 29:11 (MSG)

Write about the details of your loss. Describe what happened and how you feel.

THOUGHT TO WRITE ABOUT

Hope Thought:

    God answers "knee mail."

—UNKNOWN AUTHOR

2

HOW DO I
RESPOND TO GRIEF?

*Adversity is like a strong wind. It tears away from us
all but the things that cannot be torn, so that we see
ourselves as we really are.*

—Arthur Golden

Grief will test everything you have within yourself—and more. Until John's death brought me face to face with grief, I was just like anyone else who has not experienced it. I had no concept of the far-reaching effects of a major loss.

When grief knocks at your personal door, you *may* realize that you need to do everything possible to figure out what is happening and how to respond. (This is how I felt.) Or, like Kelly, my daughter, you may just feel utterly miserable and hopeless and not be able to think beyond that point. However, when something so devastating, unsettling, and fear-provoking invades every part of your life, you *eventually* figure out that in order to survive, you must try to make sense of it.

Sound dramatic? Yes. Is it true? Yes.

Unfortunately, while you probably wish grief would simply *go away*, that intruder does not cooperate.

> Grief will not just go away—you have to work *through* it.

What Is Grief and Why Is It So Important?

In their book, *How People Grow,* Christian clinical psychologists Dr. Henry Cloud and Dr. John Townsend discuss grief in a unique, but meaningful way. I wish I had known about it sooner because their explanation crystallized my thinking about grief. According to them, losses happen to us, but we must *voluntarily enter into* the painful process of grief. While their book does not focus primarily on grief, Cloud and Townsend offer special insight into why this kind of suffering is different:

> *Grief is the toughest pain we have to deal with. It is not the worst human experience, because it leads to resolution, but it is the most difficult for us to enter into voluntarily, which is the only way to get into it. The rest of our human experience just happens "to us." Hurt, injury, anxiety, alienation, and failure all break through, and we suffer. Grief does not "break through." It is something we enter into.*

Refusing to enter into grief blocks the way God has prepared for us to heal. I recently spoke with a middle-aged man named Will whose wife lost a lengthy, debilitating battle with cancer several years ago. When I first met Will soon after his wife died, he was angry, lonely, and depressed—understandable feelings for someone who recently lost his mate of many years. However, Will fiercely resisted his situation, initially and years afterward, and refused to accept his wife's death and adjust to the changes in his life.

Sadly, when I talked to Will again a couple of years later, he was still as miserable as when I met him. He used identical words as before to describe his life; his protests were still the same; and his discouraging outlook had not improved. He took for granted that he would never be happy again—and unless he *chooses to enter into* the grieving [healing] process, I fear he will unhappily live out the rest of his life. What a heartbreaking prospect.

Cloud and Townsend confirm that what we *choose to do* with grief directly relates to our ability to live a healthy, happy life in the future. I have seen the outcome of these decisions played out repeatedly, both positively and negatively, in people I know. How we handle grief is a crucial decision for each of us. From *How People Grow*, Cloud and Townsend further explain why grief is so important:

> *Grief will test everything you have within yourself—and more. But we must grieve so we can be happy again.*

> . . . *Grief is the one that heals all the others. It is the most important pain there is . . . It heals. It restores. It changes things that have gone bad. Moreover, it is the only place where we get comforted when things have gone wrong.*

> . . . *What is so special about grief? Why is it the "pain that heals"? Because grief is God's way of our getting finished with the bad stuff of life. It is the process by which we "get over it," by which we "let it go." . . . The soul is designed to finish things. It is designed to grieve . . . Cry it out, and it will get out. It will be over.*

As hard as we sometimes try, we cannot isolate grief from the rest of our experiences—because its effects inevitably spill out. We can't close grief up in a box, opening the lid every now and again to *peek* at the pain and the reality—and then quickly shut the lid and walk away. Healing cannot take place without *facing* the pain.

In the words of Christian Nestell Bovee, "*Tearless grief bleeds inwardly.*" We have to work through grief so we can release the pain and re-embrace life, people, relationships, and experiences once more. We *must* grieve so we can be happy again.

Grief does not just go away. Grieving our losses is critical to happiness and well-being. That is why grief is so important.

Each Grief Experience Is Unique

In working through my own grief, as well as helping others who are grieving, I have learned that each experience is unique. While similarities do exist, each person's grief is separate and personal.

Differences in grief occur not only because each person is unique, but also because each relationship, as well as each person's worldview and experience, is distinctive. In addition, the depth of your relationship, how often you interact with each other, and your physical nearness to your loved one can significantly affect the intensity of your grief. If your loved one was a key part of your daily life experience, his sudden absence will be especially keen.

> Grief experiences differ—and
> each griever's reactions vary.

Other matters can further complicate grief. Biological and physiological differences between males and females cause us to react and to process information in different ways—and a lack of understanding about these variations may create conflict. Extenuating circumstances connected to the death—and the resulting obstacles and challenges—can severely test one's ongoing ability to cope.

Related issues that add stress to grief are many and varied. For example, perhaps an accident complicated the circumstances of your loved one's death and other people are involved. Is there anxiety over injuries or a possible lawsuit? Are you facing unanswered details about the death? Are you troubled by valid questions about your loved one's medical care or exorbitant unsettled medical bills? Are family members at odds with each other over the funeral, the estate, or details of the will? Did unresolved problems cloud your relationship with your loved one? Each person faces a unique set of variables that define his grief.

Grief is complex. Diverse (and sometimes conflicting) factors come together to influence each person's grief journey.

Grievers' Reactions Differ

Just as differences occur in everyone's experience, each griever's reactions will also vary. For example, some people are extremely volatile emotionally while others are not; some grievers want to talk about what they are going through, but others have great difficulty talking; and some cry a lot while others cannot cry at all. Some people will stubbornly refuse to admit they are grieving, even when their emotional states are obvious to those well acquainted with grief.

Both similarities and definite contrasts exist in the experience of each person. Consider the following description of our varying responses to grief, perceptively written by Rabbi Earl Grollman. Everyone hurts because of grief, but each person reacts in his own way:

But It Hurts . . . Differently

There's no way to predict
how you will feel.

The reactions of grief are
not like recipes,
with given ingredients
and certain results.

Each person mourns in a
different way.

You may cry hysterically
or
you may remain outwardly controlled,
showing little emotion.

You may lash out in anger against
your family and friends,
or
you may express your gratitude
for their dedication.

You may be calm one moment—
in turmoil the next.

Reactions are varied and
contradictory.

Grief is universal.
At the same time it
is extremely personal.

Heal in your own way.

From: *Living When a Loved One
Has Died* by Earl A. Grollman
Copyright © 1977 by Earl A. Grollman
Reprinted by permission of Beacon Press, Boston

What Grievers Need

Grieving people want and desperately need to know that others care. They need the comforting arms of a hug. They need permission to talk, if they are ready; if not, they need the chance to be quiet. They need to have their situations and their conditions acknowledged by others, and they need someone who will compassionately share their pain.

What they are going through is earth shattering. Their world has been shaken at its very core. The grief journey is unquestionably one of the most difficult anyone will ever face.

> Grievers need to have their myriad feelings validated. They do not need advice. They do not need to be *fixed*. They simply *need to be heard*. And they need to be heard more than once.

The friend who can be silent with us in a moment of despair
    or confusion,
who can stay with us in an hour of grief and bereavement,
who can tolerate not-knowing, not-curing, not-healing
    and face with us the reality of our powerlessness,
that is the friend who cares.

—Henri J. M. Nouwen

(FROM *Out of Solitude*, AN AVE MARIA PRESS PUBLICATION)

When tragedy strikes, one involuntarily finds out how strong her character and beliefs are. Most of us have heard the illustration that we are like teabags—we don't really know what we're

made of until we're dropped into hot water. However, do not lose heart if you fail to live up to your own expectations immediately.

Sometimes we need time to get over the shock—time to pull ourselves together and remember who we really are. And sometimes, we need someone who knows and loves us to *remind* us who we really are. Then, we can begin to act with the strength and courage deep inside of us.

Each person *has* a reservoir of strength. Temporarily, we may have to dig deeper and with greater effort to find it because of the tragedy we face—but the reservoir is *still there*. And we can choose to tap into it.

Losses force us to make decisions about how we will go forward. Whenever we experience loss, we have options. And these options represent wholly opposite directions we can take. We can choose growth or regression; settle on acceptance or bitterness and blame; and hold on tight to what has been lost, or allow the loss to lead us to insights and fresh beginnings.

> No one can travel down the road of our wounds for us.
> —Robert A. Williams

Tough Decisions about "Wings" and "Weights"

At various times, certain relationships and activities may not be healthy or helpful. A friend told me about a pastor's teaching illustration he heard. The pastor suggested that we periodically evaluate our lives to determine who and what are "wings" or "weights." Are people and activities lifting you up or dragging you down?

Applying the 'wings and weights' concept to grief, sometimes grievers need to cut the cord, at least for a time, and release particular people or habits as they focus on mere survival. The separation may or may not be forever—but at least for now, it may be necessary for the griever's own mental health and ability to cope. If weights are bringing us down and hindering our situations instead of helping, we need to let go, in a gentle, loving way.

Conversely, some people hold us up in remarkable ways—and if ever there is a time we need wings, it's now. Make every effort to be around the people who lift you up. Keep them close! These unforgettable people will help you get through the difficult times.

Especially right now, do what is necessary to take care of *you*. Think about your relationships. Think about the people you know. Think about your interests and activities. Be aware, and make healthy choices in light of your well-being.

We remember the people who laugh with us.

And we especially remember the people who cry with us.

But more than ever . . .

We remember the people who pray with us.

Common (but Unexpected) Effects of Grief

Since many people do not understand grief (including first-time grievers), they see its effects

Especially right now, do what is necessary to take care of you.

and think their responses are unhealthy. They are unprepared for the avalanche of emotions, the depth of feeling, the confusion, depression, fear and vulnerability, lack of self-confidence, forgetfulness, and extreme, utter sadness.

Often, people do not expect the physical symptoms that accompany grief and are afraid they are sick, at best, or worse yet, crazy.

They may experience heart palpitations, or their chests may hurt so badly they think they are having a heart attack. They may be unable to eat or sleep—or they may want to eat or sleep too much. They may have upset stomachs, headaches, or dizziness. The physical and emotional symptoms seem endless.

Grief affects a person physically, emotionally, relationally, and spiritually . . . it affects every area of one's life. At different times during my grief, I experienced all of these effects. Given the severe upheaval brought on by grief, you can begin to grasp the importance of learning to deal with it positively.

Dangers of Unresolved Grief

When we avoid grief, its effects linger indefinitely and adversely affect us until we find resolution in a healthy way. Unresolved grief is the root of many problems people face such as divorce, other relational issues, addictions, depression, and various physical ailments. Unresolved grief is a serious matter.

Unhealed wounds turn into stumbling blocks that must be rationalized, defended, covered up, compensated for, and hidden behind—and these wounds are detriments to living well. In his book, *Healing Is a Choice*, Stephen Arterburn discusses ungrieved losses and unresolved pain. He explains it in this way:

> . . . *We must never shame a person who does not or cannot instantly feel the joy that awaits him or her on the other side of pain and agony. We must give them the kind of opportunity Jesus had to work through the pain and reality of suffering. If we do not, we push people into a place where they walk around with ungrieved losses and unresolved pain. This pain is never buried dead. It is buried alive and must be fed every day. It will drive*

*a person to eat, drink, spend money, have sex, gamble, and do a
thousand other things for relief. You must feel
before you can heal, or you will stay wounded
and in turn wound others who get too close.*

| Grief affects every
area of one's life.

John Welshons, in his book, *Awakening
from Grief,* also talks about the danger of unresolved losses over time.
Welshons writes,

> *Every loss in our lives forces us, to some extent, to reexperience
> the grief we have carried with us for all of life's unresolved
> losses.*

More than ever, since unresolved pain is cumulative, its consequences stir us to suitably deal with grief as we encounter it. To
promote healthy relationships and overall well-being, and to prevent
having to experience the pain *repeatedly*, we would be wise to do the
work of grief as losses occur.

The Power of Resolved Grief

Grief is not your enemy. If you choose, grief can become a catalyst
for healthy and positive changes. Grief can sharpen your perception
of relationships and awareness of important aspects of your own life.
Resolved grief has the power to deepen your faith and enrich your
life. But resolved grief takes time.

Growth is usually scary (regardless of its motivation) and requires
one to step into uncharted territory filled with uncertainty. The process of resolving grief is neither simple nor fast, nor comfortable.
Yet, a good outcome from your "leap in the dark" is surely doable.

God has promised to bring beauty from our ashes. But healing is *our* choice. God will not force us to accept this option, even though He wants the best for us. When we agree to our role in the process and choose healing, He will bring something worthwhile out of our deepest pain. Read the words of God's promise of love, joy, and restoration in the following verses from Jeremiah:

> *All growth is a leap in the dark, a spontaneous unpremeditated act without the benefit of experience.*
>
> *—Henry Miller*

God told them, *"I've never quit loving you and never will. Expect love, love, and more love!*

. . . I'll convert their weeping into laughter, lavishing comfort, invading their grief with joy."
                                    —Jeremiah 31:3, 13 (*MSG*)

When grief is at its worst, to say it's intense is an understatement. *Consuming* is a more accurate description. Seeing beyond the pain is sometimes impossible. But be gentle with yourself—because grief is complex and acceptance of reality takes time. Keep remembering that God *promises* restoration . . . renewal . . . and new joy.

The pain of grief never goes *completely* away—but if you refuse to give up, and if you allow healing to progress, God will bring something valuable out of your deeply painful experience.

At times, you will want to give up. I wish I could tell you otherwise, but I can't. The path is demanding, so please be stubbornly persistent and continue to travel, even if you must go slowly. Whatever you do and whatever it takes, decide not to give up.

Keep reminding yourself that something good can come out of your pain. I am living proof of this truth. And so are many others whom I know.

> Trust one who has gone through it.
> —Virgil

Until you are able to believe the truth for yourself, trust in the reality of others who have already traveled beyond where you are now. If others have made it through, so can you. If something good has happened for them, something good can also happen for you.

Grief is not your enemy.

Believe these truths.

Discuss any weights you have released or that you need to release.

Discuss any unresolved losses.

THOUGHT TO WRITE ABOUT

Hope Thought:

You will never change what you accept or allow. Don't let comfort or neglect lull you into accepting something destructive.

Everything around you may be falling apart, but if you remain strong, God will see your determination and reward your faith.

Suppressed grief suffocates, it rages within the breast, and is forced to multiply its strength.

—Ovid

3

HOW DO OTHERS RESPOND TO ME?

It is better to understand little than to misunderstand a lot.

—ANATOLE FRANCE

Grief is widely misunderstood. Until my husband died, I had never *lived with* grief. I knew people whose loved ones had died, but I was not closely involved with their losses. I saw grief from a distance, and did not see its true effects.

Grief is beyond understanding to those who have not received a personal introduction.

People who have not lived through grief will likely be unsure how to respond to you. Don't be discouraged, but be aware that you may need to tell those you love how they can help and what you need. People may make insensitive remarks that hurt you, but it's easier to dismiss the words when you know they just do not understand.

People Avoid Grief and Grievers

In general, today's society regards grief as an unwelcome visitor. You may have thought that way in the past.

People avoid grief as though it were toxic. Grief is scary. Some think it's distasteful and depressing, and if we get too close, someone else's grief may rub off on us by accident. Uncomfortable and embarrassing, we don't know what to do around it . . . or with it.

Grief is beyond understanding to those who have not received a personal introduction.

We may upset someone or cause the person to cry. So, instead, we try to avoid grievers or say nothing. To the one grieving, this encounter (or evasion) feels like rejection. It hurts. And grievers are already suffering excruciating pain.

Avoidance appears to be the absence of caring. It looks as if no one notices—or cares—about the griever's distress. He or she already feels alienated, and dodging further isolates the person. These typical reactions to grief form a sad, vicious cycle.

Acknowledge the Elephant so Everyone Can Stop Tiptoeing

People avoid grief (and grievers) *because they do not know what to do or say*. You can put others at ease, and quiet your own discomfort at the same time, by mentioning the loss and giving them permission to ask or talk about it.

Acknowledging the elephant everyone already knows is in the room will help to lighten the atmosphere around a grieving person. It's almost like taking a deep breath and then exhaling—because everyone will finally be able to relax a little and stop tiptoeing on eggshells.

The griever can simply let friends, family, or colleagues know it's okay to talk about the person who died or other type of loss. Often, the griever *wants* to talk but does not feel free to do so, and the same goes for other people. Assure them that if tears fall, not to worry that they are upsetting you. Tears are just part of grieving.

This straightforward approach proved successful among grief-group members in handling awkward first-time gatherings after the death of a loved one. *First* holidays, birthdays, and special celebrations after a death are difficult because the person's absence is so noticeable and sad. Without making a fuss, simply mention the person's name, acknowledge his absence, and let others know that tears are okay.

Bringing everyone's thoughts into the open relaxes the mood and clears the way for spontaneous sharing of joyful memories—a healthy exercise for everyone. When someone dies, you (and others) do not stop thinking about him; in fact, just the opposite occurs. These thoughts are likely in the forefront of each person's mind anyway. Memories are for sharing, and talking is healing. It gets easier as you practice doing it.

An open, honest approach goes a long way toward making everybody comfortable and breaking the "avoidance" tendency. Communication and understanding are necessary ingredients.

Grief Is Misinterpreted and Mistreated

In our culture, we give superficial recognition to death and grief—a brief nod—but nothing more. We don't even like to use the words *died* or *death*. Instead, we say our loved ones have *passed away* or *passed on;* they are *no longer with us;* or we have *lost* them.

Along with its impact, grief is sometimes misinterpreted and minimized even among therapists, pastors, and church leaders. Others' inaccurate perceptions undermine a griever's condition and hinder his healing. The profound effects of grief and the importance of resolving it are not widely recognized in our society.

Our culture is youth-obsessed, and the media bombards us with words and images reinforcing this message. We try to evade signs of aging and reminders of death, and growing old gracefully is a phrase that has lost its ring today. We worship youth and beauty—and aging is not respected here as in some countries.

Others' inaccurate perceptions undermine a griever's condition and hinder his healing.

As we try to distance ourselves from death and loss, grief frequently carries a negative connotation. By attempting to detach ourselves emotionally from death and confine it within a tidy box for someone else to deal with, often we are able to sidestep it—until it hits too close to home. Then, we have to decide how to respond.

Many of us are not acquainted with grief because we live far from our families and have never seen loved ones grieve openly. If we do see people grieve, we become uncomfortable. Fear about death surfaces. And we involuntarily think about our own mortality and the fragility of life. If we have not settled death's issues for ourselves, we certainly do not want to be in close company with others who are struggling with the same concerns.

Common Misconceptions and Unexpected Support

People who have not experienced grief think you should be over it in a few short weeks, or at most, a few short months. They want to *fix* you because if you are fixed, they can dismiss your pain and its repercussions. Fixing you allows them to relax again—because your loss is no longer causing them discomfort and worry or guilt. Don't be surprised if someone tells you it's time to get on with life before your grieving is done.

The stark reality of death can be threatening, and the awkward, surprising emotional reactions it triggers further intimidate some people. Grievers *sometimes* discover their strongest, most empathetic support comes from people they did not know before.

> Strangers will become friends, and friends will
> become strangers.
> —Author Unknown

These surprising words reflect the fact that you will encounter folks who do not know how (and do not want) to deal with death or grief. Often, the most caring people are the ones going through the same thing, so they truly understand how to help. When people connect at such an authentic, intimate level, deep friendships are forged.

At the same time, estrangements may occur when others are not able to support grievers when they need them the most. Death sometimes brings about unexplained separations between family members, with in-laws, or with friends—causing the griever tremendous pain and confusion. However, meaningful emotional ties and assistance often come from unexpected sources.

Death sometimes brings about unexplained separations.

In her book, *Healing After Loss*, Martha Whitmore Hickman poignantly describes the way grief sometimes alters relationships. She writes: "*We found that our circle of friends shifted . . . We were surprised and disappointed that people we thought were good friends became distant, uneasy, and seemed unable to help us. Others who were casual acquaintances became suddenly close, sustainers of life for us. Grief changes the rules, and sometimes rearranges the combinations.*"

Grief Changes Things

While you may not be able to understand *why* some of your relationships are now different, becoming aware that grief does alter things may prepare you to accept changes as they occur.

> People who have not experienced grief think you should be over it in a few short weeks, or at most, a few short months. Don't be surprised if someone tells you it's time to get on with life before your grieving is done.

Soon after my husband died, my mother-in-law (a widow of several years) cautioned me about the reality she ran into as a widow. I did not expect any of my long-time relationships to change at all; in fact, her comments upset and offended me. Surprised later on to discover elements of truth in her warning, I remembered her words.

The fact is that a widow (or any single person) does not seamlessly fit into a married couple's social world. The observation is just that—a comment, not a criticism or judgment. My friendships remained, but I had to build a new social life on my own.

Logically, the change in some relationships because of grief or loss is not hard to understand. But emotionally, it is not something you anticipate or easily accept. Just be aware.

Do Not Allow Anyone to Control Your Grieving

Well-meaning people will try to advise, critique, instruct, and rush your grief process. Resist any efforts by others to control the way or length of time you grieve. Women grieve differently from men, and one person differently from another. No right or wrong way exists. There is no perfect standard to go by.

While others may think they are being helpful by pointing out what *seems* obvious, they cannot see deep inside you. They do not know your heart, and they do not understand your grief. You have the *right* to grieve in your own way, so don't let anyone convince you otherwise.

Regardless of barriers or misunderstandings, you will get well as long as you keep moving forward. You are in control of your grief process, and you can guide those around you to support you in the way you need. In fact, they will welcome the guidance.

> *Resist any efforts by others to control the way or length of time you grieve.*

People close to you want to help, but often do not know where or how to start. When you let them know, you are making things better for yourself and for them.

Once people become aware, and gain a measure of understanding, they will be better equipped to help you and other grievers they meet. They will also be more prepared when, inevitably, they face grief themselves.

How have others misunderstood your grief?

How have your relationships changed because of grief?

Hope Thought:

The people who truly care will be your lifeline and your anchor.

You don't need a bunch of life preservers—but you do need at least one! They will help you get to where you're going.

I may not be there yet, but I'm closer than I was yesterday.

—UNKNOWN AUTHOR

THE ISOLATION OF GRIEF— A SOLITARY JOURNEY

To spare oneself from grief at all cost can be achieved only at the price of total detachment, which excludes the ability to experience happiness.

—ERICH FROMM

While those battling the tiger of grief need the loving support of family and friends who are willing to stand alongside them through this tough journey, grief is ultimately a solitary process.

No one can do your grieving for you.

> No one can do your grieving for you.

Each person must carry his own grief in his own way—and work through it himself. While every griever needs at least one person to whom she can talk honestly about her feelings, fears, and problems, ultimately, the work of grief belongs to her alone.

In *The Grief Recovery Handbook*, John James and Frank Cherry write: *"Neither this handbook nor any other guide or counselor, can recover you from your own grief. Only you can recover yourself."*

Further, recovery is not automatic, and indifference does not shield you from pain. But you don't have to drown in your grief.

> No one drowns just because they fall into the water.
> They drown because they stay there and don't or
> won't fight back to save themselves.
> —Stanley Cornils
> (from *The Mourning After—How To Manage Grief Wisely*)

Grief Alters Our Connections

One of the most difficult concepts for me as I wrestled with my own loss was the way in which grief had altered my connections to the surrounding world. I felt like a stranger, even to myself. How could the tragic loss of someone bring about such a sense of isolation, even with those I dearly loved?

During a grief-support workshop, a middle-aged woman named Laura described her life after losing her husband. The two of them met during their late teens, married a short time later, and had been inseparable ever since. *Every* part of their lives was tightly interwoven. Virtually all activities were done as a couple; their interests and abilities totally overlapped; and their ties to the world were as one. The relationship that *"shaped her identity, inspired her, and was the driving force in her life"* vanished when Laura's husband took his last breath.

Suddenly Laura's connections short-circuited. She no longer understood how to relate to her world because every part of her life had been intricately joined with her husband. She saw her life in terms of *we* instead of *me*, and did not know how to separate the two. In her words, their *"relationship flowed, and like water in a stream, it was a unified, inseparable, whole."* She saw their knowledge and experience over the years as becoming an *"ever-expanding and deepening shared resource."* She described them as being *"attached at the brain."*

> *I felt like a stranger, even to myself. How could the tragic loss of someone bring about such a sense of isolation, even with those I dearly loved?*

Part of her identity died along with her husband, and she was abruptly tossed into a world she no longer knew or understood. While it *resembled* her past, now she felt like a stranger in a strange land.

Emotionally, relationally, and intellectually, Laura felt incomplete and lost. Disorientation and emptiness filled each day. Dag Hammarskjold's words about finding a new passion for living express my hope for Laura:

> Pray that your loneliness may spur you into finding
> something to live for, great enough to die for.
> —Dag Hammarskjold

Isolation, Unfamiliarity, and Remapping

It is not surprising that grievers feel isolated. Previous ties to their world are now broken—and what remains is an uncertain, unfamiliar relationship to the world that must somehow be remapped in an unidentified, different way.

Everything that was once orderly, reliable, and familiar has suddenly become a jumbled mess.

Referring to the death of his wife, C.S. Lewis, in the book, *A Grief Observed,* poignantly describes the way his world changed: *"The act of living is different all through. Her absence is like the sky, spread all over everything."* Grief and loss suddenly restructure our lives and rearrange them in a foreign way.

Janis Brizendine (John's mother), who is also a widow, wrote the following poem about the confusion and unfamiliarity of a new life without one's mate:

What Is to Be?

If I am I
And we were we,
What in the world
Has happened to me?

There is no we,
What's here is me.
What's ours is mine,
I'm left with time.
Missing us, missing you—
Time when we were two.

I am still me.
What is to be?
I do not know.
My life will go.
So blows the wind . . .
Until the end.

—Janis M. Brizendine

The isolation of grief sometimes comes as a dramatic realization. A passage from *Tear Soup,* by Pat Schwiebert and Chuck DeKlyen, aptly describes this separation:

> *Grandy's arms ached and she felt stone cold and empty. There were no words that could describe the pain she was feeling. What's more, when she looked out the window it surprised her to see how the rest of the world was going on as usual while her world had stopped.*

I had similar thoughts about isolation and, at times, felt like an observer of my own life. The rest of the world was going on as though nothing had changed—but how could everyone *not even notice* that my whole world had turned upside down? Sometimes I felt as though I were inside a "see-through" box—living in the world, observing what was happening—but an invisible wall stood between me and everyone else.

Following is a journal entry I wrote during a grief-support workshop I attended. The writing was an exercise for us to explore role changes and our feelings about them:

Personal Journal Entry (1999)

Everything still seems odd. I don't feel comfortable yet with the changes. I'm no longer married, but I don't feel like a single person either. I feel somewhat out of place with all of our married friends, but cannot imagine any sort of relationship with someone else. I'm working at becoming as independent as possible, but don't feel completely at ease anywhere but here at home.

Role changes—I'm no longer a wife and a partner. I still have all the feelings associated with those roles, but now my feelings are tucked away inside with nowhere to go. I am now the sole financial decision-maker, with important decisions to make, and no one to share the responsibility in making them.

Some things haven't changed—I'm still a mom; a daughter and a daughter-in-law; a sister; a career woman; a friend; and many other roles associated with just living in this world.

It's difficult (and different) to suddenly be fulfilling all these roles without my husband, John, to share the joys and sorrows, the decisions, the work, and the play.

I feel like a fish out of water. Having been part of a couple for so many years, I don't really know how to be anything else.

> Sometimes I felt as though I were inside a "see-through" box—living in the world, observing what was happening—but an invisible wall stood between me and everyone else.

Feeling alienated because of the changes that accompanied my husband's death—as though I no longer belonged anywhere—I was confused. I didn't feel comfortable with myself or with others. I still had to function in my remaining roles, but I felt out of rhythm with the world. Struggling internally and externally (in relationships with other people), I tried to figure out how to behave in my new, unfamiliar environment. I had a lot to learn.

Feelings of Estrangement

Grievers feel like strangers, not only in relating to the world but also to themselves. Until they can work out how to restore (or modify) various connections, they will continue to feel like strangers.

Sometimes grievers painfully discover that previous links are beyond repair. New relationships and emotional bonds are subject to discovery and "trial and error"—some work out and some do not. Also, grief survivors may not want to reconnect certain ties because their values, priorities, and desires have changed.

Remapping takes time—and in the interim, grievers suffer in the solitude of grief.

Often our purpose for living changes when a loved one dies, and sometimes, we no longer believe we *have* a purpose. Estrangement and loneliness can rob us of the will to live. Force yourself to move beyond the pain to discover a new passion that gives meaning to life once more. Don't allow your life to become a tragedy because of your loss.

> Changing direction in life is not tragic.
> Losing passion in life is.
> —Max Lucado
> (from *When God Whispers Your Name*)

Personal Journal Entry (1999)

Reflections about my struggle with the loneliness of grief:

- *Silence & emptiness: A house that is brutally quiet, stripped of the magnetic energy, laughter, and adventurous spirit of John*

- *Overall discomfort and a feeling of oddness*

- *A sudden sense of being out of place—of not belonging—in places and with people where I used to feel completely at home*

- *Burdened by the weight of important decisions*

- *Socially—a "fish out of water"—who am I now? And where in the world do I turn?*

- *Lonely beyond comprehension*

- *Realization that, physically and emotionally, I am alone and on my own—no longer part of a couple*

I will never, ever forget those feelings of utter aloneness, especially the first nights after my husband died. In no way could I have imagined the crushing *weight* of pain. Even though family members were in the house with me, I felt harshly separated. Part of me seemed dead and unreachable.

Everywhere I glanced, my husband's personal belongings became stark reminders that without him, they were just lifeless "stuff." His absence was glaring, unnatural. The silence at night was more disturbing than a blaring horn interrupting a reverent ceremony. Inescapable memories sprang from everything I saw or touched or thought. And death was clearly present in my room.

I cannot think of a more meaningful word than wailing to convey my unspeakable pain during those nights. I had heard the word before, but it isn't a common word, so I never really gave it much thought. Now I would describe wailing as a raw, primal, real but unrecognizable sound that comes from deep inside your gut—a wrenching pain beyond explanation.

In no way could I have imagined the crushing weight of pain.

I will never forget those nights. I will never forget those feelings. And I will never forget the unfamiliar sound of my own pain. *Never.*

In such times, gratefully, we can trust the promises of our God who loves us beyond human understanding and will never leave us.

In times like these, we need someone strong, unchanging, and reliable to hold onto. We have the rock-solid assurance of God's love:

> And I am convinced that nothing can ever separate us from
>   his love.
> Death can't, and life can't. The angels can't, and the demons
>   can't.
> Our fears for today, our worries about tomorrow,
>   and even the powers of hell can't keep God's love away.
> Whether we are high above the sky or in the deepest ocean,
>   nothing in all creation will ever be able to separate us
> from the love of God that is revealed in Christ Jesus our
>   Lord.
>
> —Romans 8:38–39 (*NLT*)

Regaining the Will to Live

Through working with grievers, I have often found (particularly among those who lost spouses) that they have also lost the will to live. It is not that they want to die, but they cannot bear to face life without their mates. While that may sound like a contradiction, really it is not. They simply want to find relief from their deep pain and loneliness.

Thankfully, many people obtain help before they decide to act on their feelings. Numerous participants in the grief workshops have said that joining the support group saved their lives. Being with others who actually knew what they were feeling was invaluable.

Jill, a young woman in her thirties, was extremely close to her father even though she lived thousands of miles away. After Jill struggled alongside her dad through the strain and uncertainty of a long-term illness, he died. As hard as she tried, Jill could not pull herself out of the pain. She was lost in her grief. Her husband encouraged her to join the grief group, and this is what she wrote about her experience: *"My husband asked me the other day about the group. He said, 'That grief group really seemed to help you.' My reply? 'I think it saved my life.' However dramatic that may sound, I felt at the time that I was literally drowning in my grief and depression."*

Another woman wrote: *"Thank you for making me decide to live and trust God again."* Lily and her best friend, Ann, both lost their husbands within a few months of each other. They, too, said that participating in the grief group had saved their lives. Lily had been so despondent she had wrestled with the decision to stop eating. Ann had seriously considered taking two bottles of sleeping pills so she could avoid waking up again and facing her constant loneliness. The pain was almost too much for them.

> Never underestimate the power of *together*.
> Don't try to run alone!

The power of God and the strength of sharing with others who completely understand are life changing and life affirming. People cannot face grief alone—because this approach does not work. We need each other.

Some things in life are simply too difficult to face alone.

You may be tempted to close your heart to protect yourself, but the more you shut down to other people, the less alive you are. A hardened heart eventually dries up, and your capacity to feel and express emotions will be impaired. Do not do that to yourself.

Listening and Caring

The support and assurance of another person whom we trust, a person willing to take the time to listen as we talk, makes all the difference.

The following passage written by Dinah Maria Mulock Craik in her book, *A Life for a Life,* eloquently expresses the priceless value of a true friend: *"Oh, the comfort—the inexpressible comfort of feeling safe with a person—having neither to weigh thoughts nor measure words, but pouring them all right out, just as they are, chaff and grain together; certain that a faithful hand will take and sift them, keep what is worth keeping, and then with the breath of kindness blow the rest away."*

| *Talking heals.*

We need at least one person we trust who is willing to walk with us, without judgment or criticism, to be our comfort and our soundboard. We need at least *one person* who truly cares.

Talking heals. Talking *hurts* as it heals—but it does heal.

If you simply cannot talk to someone else about your pain, writing [journaling] is another way to work through your feelings and begin to release them. Somehow, you need to move your feelings from the inside to the outside, so you can begin to face them, release them, and start to heal.

> Facing it, always facing it. That's the
> way to get through. Face it.
> —Joseph Conrad

THOUGHT TO WRITE ABOUT

How have your relationships with others changed because of your grief?

How have people avoided you in your grief and how did this make you feel?

Hope Thought:

God is getting me ready for something. He never wastes pain or difficulties. And He won't just haphazardly "patch up" my life—He will purposely *change* it!

> *There is more to us than we know. If we can be made to see it, perhaps for the rest of our lives we will be unwilling to settle for less.*
>
> —Kurt Hahn

CHAPTER

··

INSENSITIVITY—OR LACK
OF UNDERSTANDING?

··

*One must always be aware, to notice—even though
the cost of noticing is to become responsible.*

—THYLIAS MOSS

You will probably be shocked to find out how oblivious others can sometimes be toward your loss. On the surface, what may appear to be insensitivity is often complete unawareness about your struggles with grief.

People almost never intend to hurt you—they simply do not understand. In fact, they don't even *realize* they are hurting you. If you are honest with yourself, you will probably have to admit that you, too, lacked understanding until you found yourself in the middle of your own grief.

If you have not experienced grief, you cannot know how it feels or what it means to grieve. So, at times, we *unrealistically expect* far too much from others, and we're hurt when they do not act the way we think they should. If they do not understand grief, they cannot possibly know what we need.

> Understanding human needs is half the
> job of meeting them.
> —Adlai Stevenson

A Lack of Awareness or Understanding

Soon after John died, I happened to be in a room with a small group when a friend's unthinking behavior really upset me.

My friend's husband had to go on an unexpected business trip, and he planned to be away for four or five days, extending through the weekend. When Cindy (my friend) found out about her husband's last minute trip, she went into a tizzy, acting as if he would be gone for weeks. She hastily set up get-togethers with friends and family for a bike ride, dinner, and the movies, and arranged a shopping date with her sister. She made an obvious issue of their short separation—and how she would fill her time until he returned.

If they do not understand grief, they cannot possibly know how it feels to grieve.

While Cindy created a stir as she drew others into her plans, I stood a few feet away, trying to stay focused on something—*anything*—else. Completely crushed, all I wanted to do was scream, "Your husband is only leaving for a few days! Don't you realize my husband has *died?* He's never coming home. How do you think I feel every single day?" I had to muster all of the composure I could pull together to stay silent and keep from crying.

Several weeks later, Cindy told me she was hurt because I did not invite her to do something the weekend her husband was out of town.

Comprehending another's behavior is often times difficult. While the outcome may not be intentional, self-centered actions prevent one from recognizing others' needs and feelings. Try not to make a harsh judgment, and remember that a lack of insight may be driving someone's behavior. If you can think about an incident in those terms, perhaps you'll have an easier time overlooking inconsiderate actions.

> When you judge another, you do not
> define them, you define yourself.
> —Wayne Dyer

Try Not to "React." Give Grace Instead

You will spare yourself a great deal of disappointment and pain if you realize ahead of time that people are unconsciously going to be insensitive. Recognize they just don't know *what they are saying* or they don't know *what to say.*

Resolve ahead of time to grant others some grace space. They do not intend to hurt you. Often, they want to comfort you, but do not know how. Try to dismiss their actions and go on. You need your energy elsewhere.

Forgiveness is freeing up and putting to better use
    the energy once consumed

by holding grudges, harboring resentments,
    and nursing unhealed wounds.

—Sidney and Suzanne Simon
(FROM *Forgiveness*)

As grief travelers, many times we are especially sensitive (*or over-sensitive*) to words and actions directed toward us. When something upsetting happens, pausing before reacting and giving others the benefit of the doubt will save ourselves tremendous pain.

Our first impulse is to strike back, get angry, and be hurt. If we can just remember to stop, talk to God, and release the steam of our emotions—rather than causing a confrontation—we will be better off. God promises to be with us always, and His power is sufficient for all things:

I pray that you will begin to understand the incredible great-ness of his power for us who believe him.

—Ephesians 1:19 (*NLT*)

Few are comfortable dealing with grief. Realizing that people struggle with their response to grievers can be beneficial and help us overlook some of their hurtful, distressing comments.

Grievers have enough to cope with apart from upsetting words that accidentally cause pain. By learning to release these thoughts and exchanges, a griever is actually helping himself.

Holding on to anger hurts the angry one, not the target.

Describe one or more insensitive personal encounter(s) related to your loss, and discuss how you felt about what happened.

THOUGHT TO WRITE ABOUT

Hope Thought:

Dark days do not last forever. Clouds are always moving, though sometimes so slowly we do not notice.

This, too, shall pass . . .

It's not what you look at that matters, it's what you see.

—HENRY DAVID THOREAU

6

. . . .

WHY AM I AFRAID?—AND
HOW DO I CONQUER MY FEAR?

. . . .

*No passion so effectually robs the mind of all its powers
of acting and reasoning as fear.*

—EDMUND BURKE

When grief is unknown territory, it holds the potential to unleash both reasonable and illogical fears—some that can be explained and others that cannot. If you feel unlike yourself right now, grief has probably taken control. Your strength remains intact, but for a time, grief overshadows and subdues it. Do not be afraid you have lost who you are forever. Parts of you are just temporarily hidden.

Fear is a major concern for grievers. But when you understand the fears and questions others have wrestled with, you will know you are not alone.

Numerous things about grief are puzzling, and certain effects of loss are hard to understand. For instance, my husband's death deflated my self-esteem and confidence. I felt like a stranger (even to myself), oddly separated from people, even those I loved. How had I changed so suddenly? Would I be alone forever? Would I be happy again? I could not explain these side effects or answer these questions, but they created fear and uncertainty within me. Many things did not make sense at the time.

When you understand the fears and questions others have wrestled with, you will know you are not alone.

Additionally, we tend to fear things we do not understand, and fear instinctively makes us think the worst. When we are uninformed about grief (or anything else we're up against), fear can cause a domino effect that overtakes our emotions, driving us to deeper levels of distress. By learning about grief, you can equip yourself with tools to limit fear's effects.

Fear holds the potential to multiply and swallow up our lives. We do not want to give it a chance to gain control and become a giant. We must look fear squarely in the face and move against it, or it *will* overtake us and consume our thoughts.

> To fear is one thing. To let fear grab you
> and swing you around is another.
> —Katherine Paterson

Many of Our Fears Are Legitimate

Some of our fears are not explainable. On the other hand, grief certainly brings up valid reasons for concern. As we work through grief, logical and legitimate questions arise. Fears we may need to deal with are:

- Will we be able to replace the emotional void created by the loss of our loved ones?

- Will we be able to handle the everyday challenges and emotional ups and downs of life?

- Will we be able to come to terms with the pain and grief?

- Will we be able to maintain enough control and focus to handle our jobs successfully?

- Will we make the right decisions?

- Can we get out of bed tomorrow?

- Are we going to lose someone else?

If one or both of our parents die, we may panic physically and emotionally at the thought of being alone. Childhood fears of abandonment or separation may surface.

Death can also create urgent financial issues that we must solve, and the accompanying alarm about surviving financially is a legitimate fear. When my husband died, instantly my household income dropped by about seventy-five percent. Regardless, I was still responsible for a mortgage payment, insurance, and all other existing debts and expenses while earning only a fraction of the income we had before. Immediate lifestyle adjustments were necessary. Discretionary spending almost completely halted, I cut back wherever I could, and carefully considered all purchases. Then I worked out my options before making longer-term financial decisions for my future.

Death can create urgent financial issues . . . and the accompanying alarm about surviving financially is a legitimate fear.

How do we deal with our fears? We do not want them to take over. We need answers.

Don't Let Fear Paralyze You

Many of us are not accustomed to being afraid—so how are we going to handle an invasive fear that touches countless areas of our lives? *Can* we handle it?

Fear can easily terrorize and paralyze us if we allow it. One of the best antidotes to fear is action. Alla Bozarth-Campbell, Ph.D., in her book, *Life Is Goodbye/Life Is Hello,* says:

> *Respect your symptoms of fear as you respect a stop sign. They are nature's way of getting your attention. Take time, look, listen, evaluate, and act appropriately. Anxiety is unfocused fear. It usually warns you that you are avoiding your true feelings.*

If we face our fears and act, in spite of them, we can break through the barriers that hold us hostage. Pay attention to your fears, and harness them as a springboard to action. Dale Carnegie recognized the need to act when he said, "*Inaction breeds doubt and fear. Action breeds confidence and courage. If you want to conquer fear, do not sit home and think about it.*" Take action.

Don't assume you have to solve everything at once. Try to focus on what you know and believe rather than what you fear.

The *first* thing I did to start dealing with my fear was pray. Usually strong and determined, I was flooded with details, decisions, and questions. I knew I needed help, so I prayed, *did what I could do* right then, and left the rest to God.

Friends showed up with resources, ideas, and assistance—often *without my asking.* The sale of our motorhome is just one example. I never had to advertise, plus I sold it for $10,000 above what we owed—in part due to a brilliant plan cooked up by a good friend. You never know where assistance will come from. God works in amazing ways.

Really, the only way out of fear is *through* it. Just start chipping away, little by little. Don't assume you have to solve everything at once. Try to focus on what you know and believe rather than what you fear. Counteract the power of fear by thinking and acting. *Refuse* to let fear overtake you.

And don't think too far ahead.

Decide What Is More Important

Healing is important. And taking the steps to get better is far more desirable than reaping the consequences when you allow fear to take over and immobilize you.

Seeking help when you need it is a sign of wisdom and strength.

If you need help, ask for it. Seeking help when you need it is a sure sign of wisdom and strength, not weakness—and it's an indication of your resolve to get better. Since grief can blur thinking, your judgment may not be clear. Consequently, other people may be in a better position than you are to evaluate your situation and impartially offer wise alternatives.

Ask for and accept help when necessary. Do what you must do. Be intentional. Make choices. Take action.

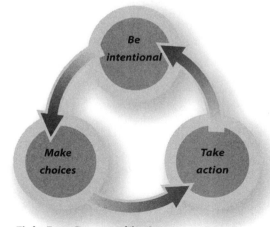

Fight Fear: Do something!

Remember, one of the best fear-fighting remedies is *action*.

Realize you *will* make mistakes. The only people who are not making mistakes are the ones who are not doing anything. Remind yourself that a mistake is not a failure—it is just a valuable lesson learned about how you do *not* want to do something next time. A mistake brings wisdom through experimentation, and while the trial-and-error method isn't the easiest way to learn, it produces wisdom all the same.

Decide to search for a path that leads where you want to go—or risk clearing a new path, a different path.

Be intentional. Make choices. Take action.

Your life is important and healing is critical. Experiment with courage. Try it on. Test it. Develop it, the same way you develop a muscle—a little bit at a time.

We must *set our minds* against fear, just as we would prepare to resist any enemy. Erica Jong's unwavering statement about her decision to move against fear is such an example. In effect, what she is doing is *trying on* courage. Notice that her fear has not vanished. She admits her fearfulness, but she *goes ahead anyway*:

> *I have not ceased being fearful, but I have ceased to let fear control me. I have accepted fear as a part of life—specifically the fear of change, the fear of the unknown; and I have gone ahead despite the pounding in my heart that says: turn back, turn back, you'll die if you venture too far.*

We *have to do* the things we're afraid to do. And we must keep doing them until we're no longer afraid. The only way to defeat fear is head-on. Stepping out, even though we are afraid, teaches us to live with passion, and this includes facing fears brought on by grief and loss.

On a sliding scale, joining a grief group can fall anywhere between mildly uncomfortable to frightening, depending on who you are. You may need a gentle push—or more of a shove—to go, but reminding yourself that a support group is a powerful tool for healing could be just the *push* you need.

> *By putting the pain to rest, you can bring the joy to life again.*

Make no mistake, deciding to enter into grief takes courage. You're moving into unfamiliar terrain, and what you encounter may be unexpected and trying. However, by putting the pain to rest, you can bring the joy to life again.

Express Your Fear

Exploring and expressing fear is not only necessary, but also crucial. Fear will not disappear just because you avoid it. In fact, it will grow larger in your mind. If you are unable to discuss your fear with a friend, talk to a counselor instead. Fear will control you unless you counteract it with action.

Test your courage. Do something.

Loss produces unknowns—and uncertainty. A couple of years after my husband died, I had to replace my car. He had always handled purchasing negotiations, and now I had to play that role. Even the thought alarmed me. So I researched *everything*—dealers' costs, options, comparative pricing, how to buy a car, etc. I organized my facts, rehearsed . . . *and brought my daughter for moral support.* I prepared! A positive outcome bolstered my courage.

Life is continually changing. And we have to keep learning and adjusting to the changes.

Sometimes luckily, and other times regrettably, nothing is forever. The physical and spiritual laws of life are not my design (or yours), and while I do not particularly like some of them, we must act within a precisely created framework. We get to choose how we live within this context, but facing the fear created by constant change is a necessary part of living and growing. John F. Kennedy said, "*Change is the law of life. And those who look only to the past or present are certain to miss the future.*"

Our world is a world of change. How we adapt is up to us.

> Do not let what you cannot do interfere
> with what you can do.
> —John Wooden

Do what you can do, as you become able. *You can always do something.* You may not be able to do as much as you would like to do, or as much as you think you should be able to do, but you can do something.

Remember, you can always do something.

We don't have to face life, grief, or fear alone—in fact we can't, at least not successfully. God did not design us to live apart from others, either in good times or in painful ones. We need each other and we need God.

We can make it, but not by ourselves. And why would we want to try?

What are you afraid of and what are you doing to conquer your fear?

What can you *do* right now?

Do you need to talk to someone about it? Fear shrinks when it's exposed to the light.

Hope Thought:

> *Courage is being scared to death, but saddling up anyway.*
>
> —JOHN WAYNE

CHAPTER

7

PIVOTAL QUESTION: DO I
REALLY WANT TO GET WELL?

*The more powerless people are, the longer they are kept
waiting.*

—MASON COOLEY

The answer to this question may seem clear. Everyone wants to get well. Don't they? The most obvious answer, however, does not tell the whole story.

Susan, a forty-year-old widow, struggled over her husband's traumatic, sudden death. Several months later, she reluctantly admitted to me that being a victim was easier than doing the hard work of grieving.

As long as a griever accepts the role of victim, he can escape the responsibility for getting well and rebuilding his life. Other people must care for a victim. He commands sympathy. A victim is powerless over the situation, helpless in controlling his emotions, and generally defenseless. Others must step in and take control because he (or she) cannot or will not do so.

You are not power-less. Becoming a victim is optional.

In effect, a victim *makes a choice* to assume the victim stance. Regardless of whether the decision is intentional or unconscious, your actions reveal your choice—and your decision propels you down a matching path.

The *choice* is yours to make. You are not powerless. Becoming a victim is *optional*.

What Will You Choose?

Devastating loss is a formidable challenge—and while you may be temporarily tempted to give in to victimhood, you will not get well by surrendering to despair.

Exercise your strength, consciously make a choice, and *do something*. Don't *allow* yourself to be a victim.

Make no mistake—working through grief is not for the faint-hearted. Choosing to be a victor is not a thought you will consider seriously (or, for that matter, will even enter your mind) when a loss first occurs. Your immediate goal is to survive—to make it through the day, or even the hour. Sometimes, the minute. But at a certain point you *will* have to make a deliberate choice about how you will face your loss.

How Do You Get Through a Tragedy?

Tragedies and difficulties are part of life, but sometimes events are beyond our abilities to explain or understand. No wonder grieving takes courage.

Unbelievable and devastating things happen that test our resolve and stun us to the core. A loved one dies in an auto or motorcycle accident. A heart attack claims a life so quickly there is no chance for medical help. An operation goes wrong. A long-term illness slowly saps the life out of someone you love. An unexpected diagnosis comes just weeks before death. A suicide or a murder traumatizes everyone in its path. Your mate leaves you for someone else. A natural disaster destroys your home and your belongings. Financial ruin takes away all your earthly security. An infant born with health problems suddenly dies, or a fetus dies before birth.

Your immediate goal is to survive . . . But at a certain point you will have to make a deliberate choice about how you will face your loss.

Does life get any tougher than this? How does anyone keep going after confronting a heartbreaking, traumatic, unexpected turn of events? What makes the difference between giving up and fighting on?

How important it is to plant the *victor* seed in your mind early! We are human beings, *not* superhuman beings, and our emotions run deep. Life is all about relationships, and when we care deeply, we do not just shake off a tragedy and keep right on going as before. However, if you plant the seed of triumph, and bring it to mind often, you will gain strength to pull yourself up and face your loss straight on.

When I was exhausted, sad, and discouraged, I stumbled. But instead of just staying down, I remembered where I wanted to go—and why.

I clearly remember a decision I made soon after my husband's sudden death, and recall my exact location when doing so. It was surely important, because more than twelve years later, I can still picture myself standing in the kitchen and making a statement that was critical to my healing. I vowed not to let what happened cause me to be bitter. And I decided to do whatever was necessary to positively work through my grief—because I did not want to let this tragedy control the rest of my life.

Did I waver at times? Yes, definitely. But that decision made early on absolutely helped me get well. When I was exhausted, sad, and discouraged, I stumbled. But instead of just staying down, I *remembered* where I wanted to go—and *why*. More than anything, I did not want to be miserable. I knew God had a life for me beyond grief.

I missed my husband terribly and mourned my loss—blatant reminders cropped up everywhere I went and in everything I did. Talking and journaling forced me to tackle my feelings head-on. I couldn't get through a church service without crying, but I went anyway, because I knew I *needed* to be there. I did things alone that we had done together.

I kept moving forward, *sometimes slowly*, but I continued facing the pain and doing the work of grieving.

> Action is critical because grief will not resolve itself.

Fighting to Go On

The sudden, untimely death of Susan's husband Tom devastated her, and for a time, she gave way to being a victim. Her entire life collapsed. His death was shocking and unexpected. He had taken care of Susan, along with everything else in their lives.

Initially scared and helpless, Susan wrestled with living alone and managing her life. She was distraught, and the overpowering pain was more than she could bear. However, she never stopped *trying* to do something.

While she struggled with her vulnerability to behave like a victim, *she did not just give up.* She kept attending a grief group. She went to counseling. She knew she did not have the strength to move forward alone, so she wisely sought help. She leaned on God.

As Susan became stronger, she reclaimed more control, but she started where she could. And in time, she made the choice to be a victor. Her decision was not a 'once and for all' decision, but a conscious choice she has had to make again and again.

I spoke with Susan not long ago and was pleased to hear about her progress—and to see the steps she is taking to rebuild her life. She found a new job. She is tackling the unfamiliar territory of household, legal, and financial duties her husband always handled before. Susan is developing a network of supportive relationships in her church, and she makes time to volunteer. She visits with family and friends, and looks for interesting outside activities to join.

> *Start where you can.*

Susan has made extraordinary steps, especially when you realize her starting point. She has taken healthy *actions* to get better. Today, she is far from a victim.

She discovered the deep truth that being a victim in her grieving was an unconscious way of holding on to her husband. Of course, it didn't work. It just prolonged her pain.

Is everything perfect now? No. Was it easy? No. However, Susan genuinely wants to get well, and she keeps moving steadily forward, growing stronger step by step.

You Always Have a Choice—So Choose Life!

When facing a loss, *you* decide what happens next. You choose how you will handle that loss. And you determine how the tragedy will affect the rest of your life.

I came across a wise statement attributed to Tony Robbins that sheds light on the importance of our decisions about how we will cope with loss. Robbins said, *"Human beings have the awesome ability to take any experience of their lives and create a meaning that disempowers them or one that can literally save their lives."*

You *always* have a choice. Will you choose life or despair? Strength or weakness? Action or immobility?

Rick and Joanne Pitino faced an unspeakable tragedy. Their baby, Daniel, entered the world three months prematurely with serious health problems. After enduring six grueling months of medical treatment and hospitalization, doctors finally released him. Then suddenly and without warning, Daniel died.

In his book, *Success Is A Choice,* Pitino perceptively writes about what it takes to carry on after something unthinkable happens. He shares his experience with the wisdom that comes from living through adversity and learning its hard-won lessons. *". . . We either learn how to overcome life's tragedies or we sink into the blackness of despair . . ."* Pitino goes on to say, *"Adversity will usually start to resolve itself when you begin to take action . . ."*

> We do not come to terms with grief by waiting for something to happen.

In time, Rick and Joanne Pitino accepted their tragic loss. They *decided* to focus on their blessings instead of what they had lost. And they looked for ways to bring something positive out of their pain. The Pitinos honored their son's memory by setting up a foundation to raise funds for underprivileged children and other charitable causes. They are generating goodness, time and again, from a heartbreaking situation.

Pitino shares more insight about dealing with tragedy in his book, *Rebound Rules.* He says, *"Tragedy will test you like nothing else*

. . . Let your emotions out, and work through them . . . Turn your grief into good . . . Don't demand answers to the inexplicable . . . Don't miss the lessons you can learn . . . Don't marinate in bitterness or preoccupy yourself with revenge."

The agony of such a reality is nearly impossible to imagine; however, each of us bears our private anguish over our losses. We do not come to terms with grief by waiting for something to happen.

Regardless of anything, you are not powerless. Of course, you need time to grasp what has happened and gain strength, but action is critical.

Choose life rather than giving in to hopelessness. Cherish your blessings instead of blaming or becoming bitter. Take action. Make choices that will enable you to rise above tragedy and become victors in spite of your pain. Others have made these choices, and so can you.

Do you really want to get well?
List some actions you are taking to heal.

THOUGHT TO WRITE ABOUT

Hope Thought:

Victor or victim? Active or passive? Bitter or better?
The past or the future? Life or death?
What do you need to change about your thinking?

I do not understand the mystery of grace—
only that it meets us where we are, but does
not leave us where it found us.

—ANNE LAMOTT

CHAPTER

8

GRIEF IS ACTIVE: THE PAIN
(AND REWARD) OF CONFRONTATION

*And the day came when the risk to remain tight in
a bud became more painful than the risk it took to
blossom.*

—ANAIS NIN

No doubt about it—grief is painful and disruptive. I have never experienced anything that interrupts life in such a dramatic way as grief. Just living life suddenly becomes a persistent struggle. Grief requires change.

Where is our equilibrium, and what is normal? Everything inside and outside of oneself is out of balance and off-course. Time seems to come to a screeching halt. And pain is pervasive.

Everywhere one goes and everything one sees (and hears) can trigger sudden reminders of the loss. On top of all that, I felt so fragile and out of control that I was completely unsettled.

Upheaval of such magnitude demands action—because who, in his right mind, would want to stay there?

Grievers have a powerful motivation to take action (once they become strong enough). One incentive for change is a personal desire to regain some sense of control, stability, and normalcy. Another stimulus is to eliminate awkward encounters with others who wrestle to contend with a griever's temporarily altered behavior. Friends or colleagues may confront you about unexpected outbursts, or a gloomy or defensive attitude.

Grief requires change.

At some point, grievers finally grow tired of their deep pain and isolation, and decide to do *whatever is necessary* to heal and restore their lives.

The drive for change will eventually override anything in its way.

While grievers cannot alter whatever has happened, and cannot transform other people, they can begin to change themselves.

So start with the changes you *can* make.

> When we are no longer able to change a situation . . .
> we are challenged to change ourselves.
> —Viktor E. Frankl
> (from *Man's Search for Meaning*)

Grief Is an Active (Not Passive) Process

Before my personal experience with loss, I held the misconception that grief is more or less a passive process. The pain would automatically lessen after a while, and acceptance would inevitably occur. It was as though I thought a griever was a patient, and eventually he would just recover—like someone who is sick, takes medicine, and then gets well.

I could not have been more wrong.

> Grief requires work, and the process does not happen without thought or effort. Time, by itself, has nothing to do with healing. And emotions do not instinctively re-stabilize.

What to Expect: Grief Travelers Speak Out

Working through grief requires gradual action. When I met her, Amy was a widow in her thirties and her only child, a daughter, was in the fourth grade. She had little time to grasp the doctor's devastating news of their rapidly approaching reality before her husband died.

Amy shared these telling words after attending a grief-support group: *"My husband passed away rather quickly from cancer seven months ago. We got the diagnosis just one week before he died. The initial shock, numbness, and disbelief are probably the hardest things anyone can endure, but I'm here to tell you that you will make it through to the other side . . . If there was a shortcut through grief, I would have found it. But the only way to recover is to walk through it one day or moment at a time. Grief is hard work, but you will feel better by taking the necessary steps."*

Another grief-group member wrote the following words (to be shared with later classes) about which every griever has thought at some point:

"You and I share something in common that no one else could relate to unless they are experiencing the loss of a loved one. Like you, I am now in the healing process of life . . .

Life is not fair, and there is no easy fix to this situation—you simply have to live through it. As much as you may not want to go on right now, life will continue. It's a hard road you must face, but please believe me when I say, in time, you will be able to look back and see that you have made forward steps toward healing.

Maybe it will be getting through one shower and not crying, or driving in your car alone and going an extra mile before the tears start to come down your cheek. Each step is a victory, a milestone, in your healing journey.

In your day-to-day living, you may feel like you're the only one going through this and asking why you were singled out. But . . . when you lift up the covers and look around, you will see there are many people feeling the same way because of a similar experience of loss.

I know this may seem impossible right now, but do not give up. You may be getting through life heartbeat by heartbeat now, but in time, it will be moment-by-moment, then minute by minute, and this time frame will continue to lengthen. It may take weeks or months, but it will get better . . .

We have experienced a part of life that everyone will face—there is no getting around this one. Keep getting up and moving forward every morning because life continues. Keep the faith . . .

You do not have to believe me right now, but in time, I think you will."

These people learned, by experience, that grief requires action, but also that healing is within reach.

One must confront grief and eventually face it in total to achieve a healthy resolution. Conversely, a Turkish proverb expresses the negative outcome when one does not confront grief: "*He that conceals his grief finds no remedy for it.*"

> Suppress grief and it stays. Face it, feel it, work
> through it, and it dissipates.

God sees your pain, and He will not leave you alone to face it. His Word clearly shows that He is aware of all you are going through. "*He will not let your foot slip—he who watches over you will not slumber . . .*" (Psalm 121:3, *NIV*). Further assurance of His presence is shown by these words of Scripture: "*The Lord watches over you—the Lord is your shade at your right hand; the sun will not harm you by day, nor the moon by night.*" (Psalm 121:5–6, *NIV*)

Take comfort in the fact that if you do your part, grief will not last forever. And you do not have to do your part alone.

Put on a "Victor" Mentality

If you can see yourself as an active participant in your grieving, you will experience a more complete, positive, and, more than likely, faster healing.

Realize that it is possible to discover renewed purpose and meaning because of working through your grief. Throw out thoughts of failure, complacency, collapse, martyrdom, passivity, powerlessness, immobility, and victimhood. Focus instead on positive emotional reinvestment in your life and on the valuable lessons you can learn through grieving your losses.

Grief can be a powerful catalyst for life-enhancing change. Make the decision to search for, and uncover, at least one thing of significance emerging from your experience.

... if you do your part, grief will not last forever.

Grief jolted me into a frank awareness that life is short and time is not guaranteed. I could never have envisioned such a tragedy happening to me—becoming a widow at forty-seven. But these things *do* happen. Life became more precious to me. And a deep desire to make a difference started budding.

Something is ahead of you—waiting for you to discover. I have heard countless stories of triumph in spite of pain and sadness.

Hope begins in the dark, the stubborn hope that if you just show up and try to do the right thing, the dawn will come. You wait and watch and work: you don't give up.

—Anne Lamott

Writing this book was a victory. Years in the making, it takes time to sift through thoughts and take hold of lessons, recall steps taken and people met, and appreciate the plain truth. Others have found new relationships and interests—and *recharged* anticipation for the future. They uncovered strengths they didn't realize they had.

Be doggedly stubborn about hope. Do not throw in the towel. Keep on going, putting one foot in front of the other, one day at a time and one step at a time.

If you don't stop, you *will* prevail.

Grief Demands a Response

> Healing requires a *committed* choice—not a vague response to leave your options open and wait to see what happens.

Subconscious thoughts and attitudes can profoundly affect healing (or its reverse). Comfort and avoidance seem preferable to, and certainly less demanding than, the pain of confrontation—but they postpone recovery.

Staying so busy that you never have the time or energy to think about your heartache does not work. When you periodically slow down and quiet your mind, reality resurfaces. Then you can process your feelings. Perhaps showing emotion is uncomfortable for you, so you stay buttoned up for fear of opening a door you can't control. *Open the door!*

Everyone facing grief wishes the options were less demanding. But even the Bible teaches us that denial does not work:

You can't heal a wound by saying it's not there!

—Jeremiah 6:14 (*TLB*)

The more proactive an individual's approach is to grief and loss, the more effective his healing will be. Grief demands a response.

When you periodically slow down and quiet your mind, reality resurfaces. Then you can process your feelings.

Do you really want to get well?
Healing hinges upon your answer.

THOUGHT TO WRITE ABOUT

How are you being "active" in your grieving?

How will you know when you are getting better?

Hope Thought:

Your future is a matter of choice—*your* choice.

The doors we open and close each day decide the lives we live.

—FLORA WHITTEMORE

9

HERE I AM, BUT WHERE DO I TURN FOR HELP AND WHAT DO I DO?

There is a sacredness in tears. They are not the mark of weakness, but of power. They speak more eloquently than ten thousand tongues. They are messengers of overwhelming grief . . . and unspeakable love.

—WASHINGTON IRVING

Suddenly, you awaken in this foreign, unfamiliar place called grief—so what happens now? The numbness and shock begin to dissipate. You feel like a stranger in your own body. You think you may be going crazy, but you do not want to tell anyone.

Grief is confusing and overwhelming.

What if you don't know anyone who has faced grief, and you have no one to help you? You probably do not understand what is happening, and you have no one to tell you what is normal.

You feel alone.

"Oh, God, what do I do now? God, are you there?"

I searched God's Word for reassurance when I was puzzled and scared. I needed help outside of myself. Grief was too big, and I couldn't fight it on my own. God promises to take care of us:

> I have cared for you from the time you were born.
> I am your God and will take care of you until you are old
>   and your hair is gray.
> I made you and will care for you;
> I will give you help and rescue you.
>
> —Isaiah 46:34 (*Good News Bible: TEV*)

Sometimes it seems as though God has forgotten us, or we mistakenly think we are being punished when tragic things happen. However, God tells us He is with us now, has always been with us, and *will be* with us throughout our lives. He affirms, repeatedly, how much He loves us. He promises to help and rescue us. Yet, of course, we would give anything to avoid the agonizing circumstances where we need rescuing.

Grief's Pain and God's Presence

In the midst of darkest pain, sometimes we must struggle to recall God's words. Sometimes we have difficulty remembering God's assurances, His promises, and His constant presence. Grief, in its early stages, is an inward look—an inner focus so intense it is hard to see or think about anything else. Anguished thoughts and feelings consume us.

The early stages of grief hold such deep emotional suffering and sorrow they defy description. My extreme emotional intensity (out of character for a person who is generally calm and peaceful) frightened me. A colleague at work even confronted me about my angry, aggressive manner.

My reactions, and over-reactions, were so foreign to my usual behavior that I actually feared I was going crazy. Strong, unexpected responses and a lack of understanding often cause grievers to question their states of mind.

> *Grief, in its early stages, is . . . an inner focus so intense it is hard to see or think about anything else.*

Without God's help (even though in the midst of pain, I had to keep reminding myself to trust Him), I would never have been able to make my way through the darkness. Without His presence and care, I would not have survived *because many times I did not want to*. I felt as though I wanted to die, but, in reality, I just wanted to escape from the unrelenting pain of existence.

Without the Grace of God, I would never have seen the positive results that finally came from the pain. God promises not to give us more than we can handle, but sometimes it seems as though He is pushing the limits. I can certainly identify with Mother Teresa's words:

> I know God will not give me anything I can't handle.
> I just wish that He didn't trust me so much.
> —Mother Teresa

Practical Support

God's presence and care act as an encompassing umbrella over His children. However, practical tools also benefit grievers. Books have always been a source of comfort, knowledge, and inspiration for me, so I began to read about grief. I started educating myself about this unknown development, this puzzle called grief. I read about the experiences of others and about the nature, obstacles, progression, and possible effects of this unfamiliar process.

Each difficult moment has the potential to open my eyes and open my heart.
—Maya Kabat-Zinn

Learning about what was happening and what to expect helped combat my fears and answer my questions.

Several months into my grief journey, I joined a grief-support group at my church. Through this group, I learned more about what grief is and how it reveals itself in grievers.

I connected with others who were traveling this unwelcome journey and quickly realized that our fears, concerns, and questions were universal. We expressed feelings and tears in a place where everyone understood and shared the same pain—a safe place where it was okay to talk and cry. We learned that grief shared really is grief diminished. Tears are undeniably healing. And through our pain, we touched each other's hearts.

Many people will not have access to a grief-support group, and others who have the opportunity will choose not to go. Attending a group is not an easy decision, especially if you are a private person unaccustomed to sharing your feelings with strangers. Jack, a man who lost his wife after a twenty-year battle with cancer, told me that he drove to a support-group meeting three weeks in a row before he built up enough nerve to go inside. Finally he did.

Participating in a support group requires courage, but the benefits are certain.

Since I had never considered attending a support group, I probably would not have joined without the prodding of my mom. When my parents came to visit several months after John died, my mother saw a notice in our church bulletin about an upcoming grief workshop. She called the leader and talked with her—and then Mom persuaded me to promise to attend the next group. I did not really want to go, but couldn't break my promise to my mom. Reluctantly, I went.

Sometimes we need a little push to do something that is tough, painful, or unfamiliar—but is for our own good.

Regardless of how independent you may be, everyone needs someone during grief.

Attending a grief-support group was one of the best things I ever did. After the ten-week group ended, several of us decided to continue meeting, and we did so for about six more months. (And to think, I didn't even want to go in the first place!) The information I learned in this group, and the opportunity to share my thoughts, feelings, and sorrow with fellow grief travelers, provided important and necessary tools that enabled me to keep working through my grief.

I discovered that talking about the loss is a healing tool, and so is crying. Learning what to expect made me less critical of others and myself when strength faltered and we mistakenly *felt as though* we had failed. And regardless of how independent you may be, everyone needs *someone* during grief.

My daughter joined the group with me (initially, she did not want to go either, but Kelly went because of me), and she attended the extended session, too. Participation forced her to deal with the heartache instead of covering it up. She saw firsthand what I was going through, and we became better equipped to understand each other's needs and hurts.

The process really works. However, you have to be courageous and vulnerable enough to attend.

Connect with Others and Allow Them to Connect with You

Finding the right words to comfort someone can be challenging, but at times, words are unnecessary.

> *When one of his classmates died, an eight-year-old friend*
> *   visited the boy's home one day after school.*
> *"What did you say?" asked his mother gently when the child*
> *   returned.*
> *"Nothing. I just sat on his mom's lap and cried with her."*
>
> —Applewhite, Evans, and Frothingham
> (FROM *And I Quote*)

Sometimes, the presence of someone who genuinely cares is the *only* thing needed. Words become unimportant. Empathy, direct eye contact, and the touch of another human being speak volumes all by themselves.

When we are hurt, our natural tendencies are to withdraw, and grief likely presses us toward isolation unless we really fight against the urge. If we build walls and try to keep people away whenever we are in pain, our lives will undoubtedly be bleak and lonely.

Grief likely presses us toward isolation unless we really fight against the urge.

God did not create us to live life on our own. And unless we share our grief with others, we will never completely heal. In addition, our bodies are not engineered to carry pain inside without a means of letting it go. Unless we learn to release emotions, our bodies will eventually suffer—and the stress will reveal itself in some tangible way.

We *need* to connect with others, but we also need to *allow them* to connect with us. We may or may not remember someone's words— but I guarantee we will remember genuine moments of contact.

> They may forget what you said, but they will never forget how you made them feel.
> —Carl W. Buechner

You Have to Face the Pain

The only effective way to face grief is head-on. You cannot go over, under, or around it—you must walk *straight through it.* I remember my grief-group leader saying these words the first

The only effective way to face grief is head-on.

night we met, and I've repeated them to myself and others countless times.

Of course, most people in pain want to do whatever they can to escape it. Wanting to feel the pain is unnatural; however, unless you do so and work through it, the road to healing short-circuits and leads to a dead-end.

Sharing grief does help you heal, and lessens your burden of pain. In leading grief-support groups, I have found this concept to be true. A group member wrote:

> *"I didn't realize how much of an effect the sessions had until I was unable to attend the last two and very much missed them . . . I, personally, will never get over the tragedy that has occurred, but . . . your guidance, caring, love, and sharing have already*

started me on the road to acceptance and moving on with my
life. I have shared much of what I received with my two sons,
and they in turn are using all of that stuff to move on.

I also want to thank everyone in the group for being a part
of my life and sharing your thoughts and grief with the rest of
us. We each have our burdens, but sharing around the table with
others in different ways made them gentler and maybe somewhat
more acceptable."

Our Responses Make All the Difference

Adversity is part of life. While we have no choice as to most of
the obstacles we face, we do get to choose our responses—and our
responses *direct* our lives.

What type of catalyst are you putting in motion: A positive or
negative one? A bridge or a roadblock? Faith or fear? Your choice triggers a series of reactions.

> Our lives are not determined by what happens to us
> but by how we react to what happens, not by what
> life brings to us, but by the attitude we bring to life.
> A positive attitude causes a chain reaction
> of positive thoughts, events, and outcomes.
> It is a catalyst, a spark that creates extraordinary results.
> —Anonymous

We do not have to fight adversity alone. As children of Almighty
God, we have the *power of the universe* available to us. As Max Lucado
says in *The Great House of God:*

What controls you doesn't control him. What troubles you doesn't trouble him. What fatigues you doesn't fatigue him. Is an eagle disturbed by traffic? No, he rises above it. Is the whale perturbed by a hurricane? Of course not, he plunges beneath it. Is the lion flustered by the mouse standing directly in his way? No, he steps over it. How much more is God able to soar above, plunge beneath, and step over the troubles of the earth!

Amen! Keep your eyes focused on the source of your power and hope—not on your circumstances. Also, remember what He can do.

Keep Going until You Can Choose to Live Again

Often, during adversity, we must remind ourselves to keep going. Many times, we want to give up. But if we hang on, at some point, the *life* vision, the "dreams" resurface—and we *make the decision* to live again. This response is a pivotal point in our healing. Life wins out over death.

Initially, a dream may be only a shadow, a seedling, a spark of what is to come . . . but it's conceived out of *something* resonating deep within your soul, something calling out to you *to live.*

> *A dream is an evolving concept that changes form and direction as you go, inspiring you to take a risk.*

What do you keep thinking about and going back to continually? What excites you? What do you long to achieve? What do you love to do? Whom do you want to help?

Your dream does not have to be highly honed or fully formed to take shape. A dream is an evolving concept that changes form and direction as you go, inspiring you to take a risk doing something worthwhile, to look for the finest fruit at the end of the skinny branches, and to go where you are afraid to go.

Norman Vincent Peale said, *"Throw your heart over the fence and the rest will follow!"* Listen to the deep longings of your heart and follow wherever they lead—in spite of your fear. Do that and you won't ever have to wonder whether you have really *lived.*

Dare to live your life in the bright sunshine of action and discovery, not the murky twilight of indecision, self-doubt, and procrastination. Listen to your heart . . . and take the first step toward your dreams.

I love Mark Twain's spirited call to step out and *live!* Twain writes: *"Twenty years from now you will be more disappointed by the things that you didn't do than by the ones you did do. So throw off the bowlines. Sail away from the safe harbor. Catch the trade winds in your sails. Explore. Dream. Discover."*

I urge you to get back into the sea of life. Dream your dreams. Sail your vessel. Get out of the safe harbor of your comfort zone. *Take chances.*

Live life again—and make it the best of your life thus far. With God's help, your future is limitless! Respond to the challenge.

> Promise me you'll always remember: You're braver
> than you believe, and stronger than you seem,
> and smarter than you think.
> —A. A. Milne

Describe a dream for your future.

What *one step* can you take today?

Hope Thought:

You and God are the majority! Is your "want to" big enough? If you weren't afraid of failing, what would you love to try?

Dream big! Think about it . . . but don't just think about it, *do* it!

> *Before they call out, I'll answer.*
> *Before they've finished speaking, I'll have heard.*
>
> —Isaiah 65:24 (*MSG*)

10

"JEEPING" OVER
UNKNOWN TERRAIN

Turmoil

My life is in turmoil,
Like March.
Sudden storms,
Sudden spring days,
Sudden tears
And laughter.

—Janis M. Brizendine

John owned one of the older "real" Jeeps [as a diehard Jeep enthu-siast would say]—a CJ-7. He was like a little kid with a brand new toy on Christmas morning. The Jeep was his outlet for adven-ture. He loved to go off-road where travel was bumpy and obstacles were simply an anticipated challenge. In off-roading, the terrain was uncertain. Bumps were common and could be fierce.

A couple of weeks before he died, John went jeeping with friends in the California desert. He slowly and carefully edged his way through a giant rock pass. The opening was so narrow that people sat atop the rock formations on both sides and kept the vehicle from scraping the rocks by pressing their feet against it to maintain clearance. He was so proud of having conquered this treacherous pass! However, he could not have done it alone.

A mental picture similar to that of jeeping can represent grief. The path is bumpy, and the obstacles are challenging. In grief, as in jeeping, the path and terrain are uncertain. Often, we come very close to scraping ourselves on the jagged rock edges—and sometimes we actually do, because we just cannot stop it from happening. The many ups and downs will frequently take us by surprise.

Sometimes we have no idea what is happening to us—or why.

Controlling Emotional Chaos

Grief, by its very nature, is a disorderly process. Tangled emotions threaten to strangle us at times as we struggle to control our out-of-control emotional roller coasters. Now and then, total upheaval and chaos reign. Nevertheless, we must *learn* to be gentle with ourselves.

The grief journey is certainly a back-and-forth, uneven path to an unfamiliar destination. We take one step forward, followed by two or three steps back. We advance slowly, and then we suffer a stunning blow as we suddenly collapse on our knees or fall flat on our faces, yet again.

> *Our greatest glory is not in never falling, but in rising every time we fall.*
> —Confucius

Recognize (*and remember*) that this jagged path is actually not a *regression* in our healing journeys, but a *progression*—and simply part of the process. You *are* getting better, so try to be patient with yourself. What is important is to get back up and keep on going.

> An erratic journey is the reality of grief. Learning
> what to expect can free us to experience the process,
> work through the pain, see beyond it—and stop
> beating ourselves up when we tumble down.

Sometimes we have to struggle to gain control over our emotions because if we do not, our emotions will rule our lives.

We must take action—or more specifically, *counter-action*—to regain control and change direction instead of giving in to an emotional state we do not want to occupy. We may need to laugh when we don't feel like it. Or act even though we are frozen with fear. Or remember we are God's handiwork when we are hypercritical of ourselves.

Episodes of feeling sorry for oneself are common responses to loss, and falling into that mindset is easy. I was no different. Luckily, I generally caught myself before sinking too deep (or someone reminded me) and I stopped. Instead, I switched gears toward counting my blessings—my beautiful daughter who needed me, family and great friends, God, a satisfying job, and more. Before long, my *counter-action* worked! Negative and positive emotions can't occupy the same space simultaneously—at least not in my experience.

With God's Help, We Have Power

We are far more powerful than we realize. During grief, we would do ourselves a favor if we reflected on things that remind us of our strengths rather than our weaknesses. Try to stay focused on positive, life-affirming, faith-building ideas and truths.

My thoughts keep returning to God because He is the way, the only way. Without the Grace of God, I would never have escaped the darkness of my grief.

Prayer changes things. Prayer changes us.

A relationship with God gives a believer access to greater power than we can conceive. Prayer changes things. Prayer changes *us*. I once heard a pastor refer to prayer as the "love child" between God and His church. That illustration expresses how precious our prayers are to Him. God does not pass over prayers of faith.

> The prayer of a person living right with God is something powerful to be reckoned with.
>
> —James 5:16 (*MSG*)

Read the following thoughts from grief-support-group members, describing God's help in facing their journeys:

One lady wrote, *"We need to let go and let God help us. He will show us the way."*

Another person said, *"Cry out to God for help and watch how He shows himself."*

A young man who lost his wife shared, *"What I have learned the most these past ten weeks is that I have a great shepherd . . . therefore, I will not fear. The Word of God is true . . . God is faithful."*

Someone else wrote: *"If you do not have a belief system, please find one because this will aid in your healing. If your belief is in God, rest assured He will be there for you, even when you're blaming Him. God is good."*

Still another said, *"You are not alone . . . others have gone this way before you . . . God is with you . . . even if you don't always feel him."*

Finally, a widow wrote, *"Be still and know that I am God. In all your worries, sorrow, and anxieties, be still . . . and know that I am God . . . GOD. God brings peace to me in this verse."*

In the Bible, we read about the availability of the ultimate power, the Holy Spirit—God living in the believer. *". . . if anyone is in Christ, he is a new creation; the old has gone, the new has come!"* (II Cor. 5:17, *NIV*); *"My grace is sufficient for you, for my power is made perfect in weakness."* (II Cor. 12:9, *NIV*); *"Now to him who is able to do immeasurably more than all we ask or imagine, according to his power that is at work within us."* (Romans 3:20, *NIV*). God's power is limitless.

> *When life knocks you to your knees—well, that's the best position in which to pray, isn't it?*
> —Ethel Barrymore

The Power that created the universe, raised Jesus from the dead, and spread Christianity throughout the world in spite of persecution and hardship—is the same power that is available today! When God works His power through you, *anything* is possible—and nothing is beyond your reach.

Remember, with God, limits are nonexistent. His power is always available to His children, but it is more apparent when we are weak—because that is when we need Him the most.

When we look for Him, He will not fail us. In His Word, He promises to be faithful to us. And countless stories of believers testify to God's presence and help during their times of desperation.

With Him, we can face anything—any problem, any adversity, any circumstance. His power is most evident to us then.

He gives strength to the weary and increases the power of
    the weak.

Even youths grow tired and weary, and young men stumble
   and fall;
but those who hope in the Lord will renew their strength.
They will soar on wings like eagles; they will run and not
   grow weary,
they will walk and not be faint.

—Isaiah 40:29–31 (*NIV*)

When God works His power through you, *anything* is
possible—and nothing is beyond your reach.

What are some of the "bumps" (or challenges) you have encountered? How have you handled them?

Hope Thought:

If God had a bulletin board, your picture would be on it.

He sends you flowers each spring, sunrises every morning, and rainbows as reminders of his love.

He could live anywhere, but He chose to live in your heart.

The God of the universe is your loving father—and He is crazy about you!

You are His treasure. You are His masterpiece. You are His precious child.

He *loves* you . . . no matter what!

God loves each of us as if there were only one of us.

—St. Augustine

ANGER, GUILT, DEPRESSION, AND "WHY?" QUESTIONS

Anger is really disappointed hope.

—Erica Jong

Anger

At least sometime during the grieving process, people are angry with doctors, their family, God, their situation, themselves—and even with the person who died.

Clearly, not all anger is rational, and can cause us to make decisions we will later regret. While anger is normal when working through grief, if it lingers too long or harms others emotionally or physically, it is obviously not healthy—and can be destructive.

I have encountered people in grief-support groups who did not even realize they were angry until they started to journal or talk about what was on their minds. As they faced their feelings and began to identify them, anger percolated to the surface . . . and they recognized its presence lurking within their own issues. This realization enabled them to work through the anger and move toward healing.

Carrie's mom died after a long illness. Their relationship had been a tug-of-war for control throughout their lives, but the two of them worked hard to resolve their differences before her mom died. Carrie wrestled with guilt and deep sadness over her mother's death, and she withdrew, internalizing her loss.

Anger: an acid that can do more harm to the vessel in which it is stored than to anything on which it is poured.

—Seneca

As she discussed her situation, Carrie grew angry. She blamed her husband for not being supportive. However, she had not shared any of her feelings with him. He had no idea what was going on, what she needed, or how he could help. Carrie's withdrawal had pushed him farther away. Once she realized what was happening, she knew that their issues were the result of her unidentified (and unjustified) anger. She saw that she needed to communicate with her husband and begin to release the angry emotions.

I have encountered people . . . who did not even realize they were angry until they started to journal or talk about what was on their minds.

Anger can actually help us. It can bring us to the point when we finally say, "Enough is enough," and we *decide* it is time to do whatever is necessary to get better. Anger reminds us, after feeling numb, that our emotions are reawakening.

Anger reminds us we are still alive.

In the following poem, *I Told God I Was Angry*, Jessica Shaver Renshaw speaks honestly about thoughts we may have but are tough to admit, even to ourselves.

Anger toward God can be difficult to face up to because it generates tremendous guilt. Sometimes anger focuses on others or even on oneself, but regardless of its target, confession and forgiveness are necessary.

I Told God I Was Angry

I told God I was angry.
I thought He'd be surprised.
I thought I'd kept hostility
quite cleverly disguised.

I told the Lord I hate Him
I told Him that I hurt.
I told Him that He isn't fair,
He's treated me like dirt.

I told God I was angry
but I'm the one surprised.
"What I've known all along," He said,
"you've finally realized.

"At last you have admitted
what's really in your heart.
Dishonesty, not anger,
was keeping us apart.

"Even when you hate Me
I don't stop loving you.
Before you can receive that love
you must confess what's true.

"In telling Me the anger
you genuinely feel,
it loses power over you,
permitting you to heal."

I told God I was sorry
and He's forgiven me.
The truth that I was angry
has finally set me free.

> —Jessica Shaver Renshaw
> © 1989

Anger is a normal response to loss. However, anger victimizes us. Just like all other emotions connected to grief, resolving these feelings constructively promotes mental and physical health.

In Patsy Clairmont's book, *Under His Wings,* she talks about the importance of experiencing the full range of emotions connected with grief:

> *If we don't feel, weep, talk, rage, grieve, and question, we will hide and be afraid of the parts of life that deepen us. They make us not only wiser but gentler, more compassionate, less critical, and more Christlike.*

Unless we squarely face the difficult, painful parts of life, we will not go through the steps that give us the capacity to be more deeply human. Grief work is worth the price.

Guilt

Most people (actually, all!) feel guilty and try to second guess what they coulda, shoulda, might have done . . . and on and on. Truthfully, most people do the very best they can with what they know at the time. Maya Angelou talks about making mistakes and doing better:

> It is very important for every human being to forgive herself
>   or himself because if you live,
>   you will make mistakes . . .
> But once you do and you see the mistake, then you forgive
>   yourself and say,
>   'well, if I'd known better I'd have done better,' that's all.
>
> —Maya Angelou

We can all look back, and with the advantage of hindsight, form different judgments and other conclusions—but that serves no purpose except to make us feel guilty. Let it go!

Guilt is one of Satan's most powerful tools of deception. Genuine (healthy) guilt can ignite our consciences when we have done something wrong and alert us to the need for confession to God. However, Satan uses guilt to weave a web that leaves us feeling rejected, isolated, confused, demoralized, frustrated, punished, unforgiven, worthless, ashamed, and condemned. This unhealthy, *accusatory* guilt can cause us to believe we have drifted too far from God to return.

> *Remember that we can never drift too far from God's love and grace.*

Satan's use of guilt can make us doubt the sincerity of our relationship to God. It is like a deadly cancer, and left unchecked, can invade our lives, spread, and wreak devastation in many areas. Remember that we can never drift too far from God's love and grace. According to God's Word, we do not have to live in guilt:

> God is faithful and reliable. If we confess our sins, he forgives them and cleanses us from everything we've done wrong.
>
> —I John 1:9 (*God's Word*)

But positive steps combat the effects of guilt. Prayer and confession are essential because they lead to forgiveness and a clear conscience. This approach is a constructive way to handle guilt, and the same is true for talking to a trusted friend or writing a letter to the person who died. Releasing the feelings, and getting past the "should have" syndrome, are vital defenses against guilt.

Conversely, allowing your thoughts to perpetuate guilt (by labeling yourself as bad, wrong, weak, hopeless, or a failure) is a detrimental, unhealthy action that allows Satan to deceive you and keep you from accepting God's forgiveness.

Decide to handle guilt in the way that leads to peace and freedom—God's way.

Depression

Depression forms the last part of this insidious emotional triangle. We work through the emotions associated with grief as we identify, express, and release our feelings. Becoming more aware of our thoughts and resisting the urge to dwell on the negative helps to combat a mindset that fuels depression. We tend to forget or do not realize how extraordinarily powerful thoughts are. Our focus will send us in a particular direction—positive or negative, healthy or unhealthy.

When we think of depression, we generally connect it to feelings of apathy and other physical and emotional symptoms that interfere with our daily abilities to function and enjoy life. Common symptoms of depression may include the following:

- Inability to enjoy activities that were once pleasurable

- Changes in eating and sleeping patterns

- Fatigue

- Restlessness and anxiety

- Difficulty concentrating, making decisions, and remembering things

- Withdrawal from people close to us

- Extreme guilt and feelings of hopelessness

- Preoccupation with thoughts of death or suicide

While many of these are normal responses to grief, if the symptoms continue without improvement for several weeks, or highly interfere with your ability to function, consult a medical professional for evaluation and help.

Do not suffer needlessly when treatment and relief are available. Depression is an illness, not a sign of weakness or a cause for humiliation.

A serious, but less recognized form of depression, reveals itself by the absence of feelings. When one experiences an ongoing sense of detachment and a general "deadness" inside that does not go away, these indicators also signal the need for professional help. The longer these symptoms linger and intensify, the deeper into depression one sinks. Often, the assistance of a professional therapist is necessary to help unlock the emotional shutdown.

Seeking help is not shameful. In fact, acting on the desire to find professional help is a step in the right direction. Getting help is a sign of assuming responsibility to get better, and taking this action puts one in the victor rather than the victim position.

Forgiveness

Unforgiveness causes guilt. And unforgiveness will not only hurt us, but will keep us from being in a right relationship with God.

Forgiveness is a choice, a decision, an action. It is not a feeling. And forgiveness is a *command* from God, not an option.

> In prayer there is a connection between what God does and
> what you do.
> You can't get forgiveness from God, for instance, without
> also forgiving others.

> If you refuse to do your part, you cut yourself off from
> God's part.
>
> —Matthew 6:14–15 (*MSG*)

God does not ask us to forgive because someone deserves forgiveness—but because He forgave us. I have heard several pastors explain the concept, and it is easier to understand (and accept) when you realize forgiveness releases a legitimate debt *that cannot be repaid.*

Forgiveness releases a rightful debt that cannot be repaid.

Forgiveness sets the prisoner free—and this insight is especially significant when you recognize *the prisoner is you.*

I will never forget the first time I heard the truth about forgiveness taught from this perspective. The revelation was an *Aha!* moment of dramatic proportions. Realizing we sometimes allow ourselves to be held hostage by hanging on to a *rightful* debt that *cannot* be repaid was a monumental concept—and a liberating truth. Forgiveness is the key.

Unforgiveness destroys our hearts because most of the time, the person we cannot forgive is completely unaware. We are harming ourselves. *We* are the prisoner we need to set free.

> He who cannot forgive breaks the
> bridge over which he himself must pass.
> —George Herbert

Why???

In grief-support groups, I have seen people so entangled by "Why?" questions they cannot get beyond this point. "Why?" becomes a tremendous obstacle to healing.

Occasionally, circumstances of the death automatically generate questions; however, I respectfully suggest that the *why* really is not important. If you knew why, would you grieve less? Would anything change? Would knowing why honestly make a difference?

Most of us will never find the answers to our "why" questions here on earth.

We can trap ourselves by endlessly questioning God about our conditions, His actions, and everything else. Questions that drive us to dig deeper and find answers to strengthen our faith are a different story—these are beneficial. While questions such as, "Why have you allowed this to happen to me?" and, "Don't you love me anymore?" and, "Have you forgotten me?" are thoughts that have crossed my mind, and possibly yours—*getting stuck here is a trap.*

Faith is the bottom line. Are we trusting God or not? Will He take care of us or not? Does "why" really matter?

> The "why" of so many things is sometimes known only to
> the heart of God.
> But He has promised us . . . that at all times, in all places,
> and in all circumstances,
> nothing can separate us from His love.
>
> —Author Unknown

The Bible teaches that before we were born, God numbered [determined] our days (Psalms 139:16). While not everything that happens to us is necessarily God's will, nothing happens that He does not see and permit. Therefore, asking God what He wants to teach us from our situations rather than why we are there is much healthier—because He has our best in mind. Perhaps we should ask God how He wants us to use what we have learned.

You are not alone.

God will grow us where we are—if we will surrender to Him. And isn't placing our trust in God through *all* our circumstances what is most important? Of course, these actions are not easy. But He will be with us. He promises.

When sharing my journal writings in grief groups, I invariably found that people related to what I had written about my journey. Often the writings helped them identify concepts and feelings they had been unable to express.

After hearing my journal thoughts read aloud, one group member wrote, *"Nothing feels like having someone put into words what you cannot articulate, but feel so deeply; to hear your thoughts spoken by others and know you are not crazy; to tell your story to others who know better what you are going through than anyone else could."*

You are not alone. While each grief experience is unique, our feelings of loss are universal. Perhaps you will be able to recognize some of your own feelings as you read about mine.

Personal Journal Entry, 1999:

I've thought a lot about my life since John died, about how I feel and how everything has changed so drastically.

At first, there was just numbness and a complete sense of unreality—that this awful thing couldn't be true . . . that it was a bad dream, and sooner or later I'd wake up and everything would be okay. But it wasn't a bad dream—it was real. And reality was a shocking sense of loss; unrelenting emptiness and loneliness; and the realization that I had lost a priceless treasure.

My husband, John, had a pure exuberance for life! I've never known anyone who had more zest for living. He delighted in life, and his delight was contagious. He had an energy that sparked others to participate. He had a joyful, playful personality and he easily made friends.

People trusted him because he was honest and trustworthy. John was very real. There were no pretenses—and you always knew where he stood. He spoke up for what he believed, even when doing so was uncomfortable or it was safer to remain silent. He believed in doing the right thing. He would have done anything for his friends.

John had such a powerful personality that his absence is unmistakable. We were very different. He was so many things that I am not, and vice versa. I feel as though a big part of me disappeared with him.

I feel guilty for taking many things for granted. Maybe I wasn't grateful enough. I wish we could go back, but we can't.

The future is uncertain and scary. I've never been completely on my own before. I have to make decisions by myself that I don't like making.

I get angry that people, even some friends, can be so unaware. Doesn't anybody understand?

The Lord has left me here for now, and I can't stay trapped in depression and anger and all those negative feelings—and I can't hang onto the past and live there. I have to live here and now. I don't know what that means, but I have to trust God to show me.

I want to begin to heal. With God's help, I will.

Grief stirs up our emotions, and brings fears and uncertainties to the surface. It is easy to get hopelessly entangled by our worries about the future, but as much as we may feel alone, we're not. God promises to help us with whatever we have to face.

> Don't get worked up about what may or may not happen
> tomorrow.
> God will help you deal with whatever hard things come up
> when the time comes.
>
> —Matthew 6:34 (*MSG*)

Surrender is a necessary step toward healing, but surrender does not mean forgetting the person or the past. Surrender *does* signal a griever's acceptance of the loss. With accep-tance, one begins to focus on reinvesting in the future—and living again.

Surrender does not mean forgetting the person or the past.

Setbacks will certainly occur, but an aware-ness of the future begins to replace an overall preoccupation with the loss.

We Have a Purpose for Being Here

Here is the test to find whether your mission on Earth is finished: if you're alive, it isn't.
—Richard Bach

We can be certain that if we are still alive, God has a reason for our being here. When He created us, God made us for His purposes—as part of His intricate overall design. As long as He has plans we are instrumental in carrying out, our lives on earth will continue.

We can also trust that God's purposes for us are perfect. He knows us better than we know ourselves.

Describe your struggles with anger, guilt, depression, and "Why?" questions. If you still need to forgive someone, talk about it.

How are you beginning to surrender? What are your thoughts about the future?

Hope Thought:

Focus on God, not on your circumstances.

When Satan pressures you, ask him if he knows who your Father is.

Satan can disturb us, deceive us, tempt us, distract us, and confuse us, but he cannot defeat us. We have God on our side.

> *Indeed, one step taken in surrender to God is better than a journey across the ocean without it.*
> *Perfectly to will what God wills, to want what He wants, is to have joy;*
> *but if one's will is not quite in unison with God's there is no joy.*
> *May God help us to be in tune with Him.*
>
> —MEISTER ECKHART

12

. . . .

EMOTIONS: A MISLEADING
AND UNRELIABLE GAUGE

. . . .

*Feelings are not supposed to be logical. Dangerous is
the man who has rationalized his emotions.*

—DAVID BORENSTEIN

Using emotions to gauge the reliability of *anything*—especially
something spiritual—is not only foolish, but also dangerous.
All of us have fallen into the trap of forming, examining, and changing our perceptions based on emotions. But when we use emotions as
a tool to assess God or our spiritual lives, we are headed for disaster.

In his book, *When God Doesn't Make Sense*, Dr. James Dobson
graphically observes: *"Not only is human perception a highly flawed
and imprecise instrument, but our emotions are even less reliable. They
have the consistency and dependability of Silly Putty."*

During grief, emotions propel us into high gear. What if we do
not *feel* God's presence with us? At a time when we need Him most, if
we begin to believe God is not with us just because we don't feel His
presence, we are headed for trouble. Staying grounded in spiritual

truth and affirming the promises of God through His Word keep us on a secure path, nourish our faith, and protect us from deception.

If we believe God is not with us just because we don't feel His presence, we are headed for trouble.

Take some practical steps to counteract your inaccurate, unreliable feelings. Look up some of God's promises in the Bible, write them out on note cards, post them on your bathroom mirror, put them in your briefcase, handbag, or in the console of your car, and read them to yourself several times a day. Better yet, find a favorite promise about God's presence, memorize it, and repeat it to yourself daily.

Actively work to replace spiritual deception with God's truth.

We Can't Escape from God's Presence and Care

Grief is an exceptionally vulnerable time. Initially, when our focus is pinpointed within ourselves, struggling with confusing feelings and pressing issues, it is easy to become hopelessly entangled in our emotions.

Remember that God is always at work on your behalf, even when you cannot see any evidence. He is always with you, even when you do not feel His presence. He will protect and take care of us—*whether we see or do not see.*

Stay focused on the truth . . . and stay focused on His love. We are God's workmanship, His masterpieces, His treasures. He made us for a purpose and to love us, to have relationships with us—so will He then abandon us? Impossible!

> Where can I go to get away from your Spirit? Where can I
> run to get away from you?

If I go up to heaven, you are there. If I make my bed in
  hell, you are there.
If I climb upward on the rays of the morning sun
    or land on the most distant shore of the sea where the
    sun sets,
even there your hand would guide me and your right hand
    would hold on to me.

—Psalm 139:7–10 (*God's Word*)

Joyce Meyer, in her book *Managing Your Emotions*, talks about emotions and how they relate to spiritual decision-making. Meyer writes that, as humans, we are wired with emotions. However, we can *learn* to manage our emotions *and recognize* that we can't trust them. Satan will try to use them against us. Meyer says, "*I have read that when emotion pulsates, the mind becomes deceived, and conscience is denied its standard of judgment.*"

Meyer tells us that a way to test our emotions is to "*learn to wait.*" Emotions tend to push us toward a quick response. On spiritual decisions, Meyer cautions us to wait until we have clear direction as to "*what it is we are to do and when we are to do it.*"

If we can "*develop the capacity to back away and view our situations from God's perspective,*" then we will learn to make decisions "*based on what we know rather than on what we feel.*"

If Possible, Postpone Major Decisions

During grief, emotions are especially untrustworthy in decision making. Sometimes we make impulsive decisions because we hope the change will enable us to feel better and lessen our pain. If possible, however, by delaying major decisions until we have time to regain equilibrium, sort out the facts, and think more clearly, our choices will be guided by reason instead of hastiness for change.

Within days of his wife's death, Jack quickly cleared her clothes from their closet and arranged to dispose of his wife Diane's belongings. Her twenty-year illness challenged their family, emotionally and physically, and he had already grieved for years before she died. So he was anxious to release the past and start fresh.

In his rush to move forward, Jack almost gave away several of Diane's belongings that were irreplaceable and of great sentimental value, one being her wedding gown. A new beginning did *not* mean wiping the slate clean. He treasured the memories of their lives together. Luckily, Jack discovered his slip-up as he checked the boxes right before sealing them.

During grief, emotions are especially untrustworthy in decision making.

Many sources recommend waiting at least a year before making significant, life-changing decisions such as selling your home and moving (possibly even to a different town or state), changing jobs or careers, remarrying, or making major financial decisions.

Obviously, sometimes you have no alternative but to go ahead and act, even though waiting would be preferable. Perhaps your financial situation forces the sale of a property. Or maybe an illness requires a job or career change. If you have no choice but to make a major change soon after your loss, with the support of trusted friends, family, and advisors, you will be compelled to deal with the necessary changes the best way you can.

When you do have an alternative to making important changes too soon, wait. I have known a couple of widows who sold their homes and moved to a different state very soon after their husbands died because they believed the change would be positive. Instead, both of them were extremely lonely. They deeply regretted their decisions and eventually returned to their original locations.

Grief can be even more difficult to handle when a griever must face numerous losses all together. One middle-aged couple moved cross-country when he retired so they would be closer to their children. However, soon after they relocated, the husband, Scott, became ill and died. Scott and his wife, Anne, had been active, longtime residents of their previous community and had established deep ties there. Their church was an important part of their lives, and they were very involved. Sometime after her husband died, as Anne was going through the grief process, she realized she was grieving not only the loss of her husband, but also the loss of her home, church, familiar surroundings, and lifelong friendships. The string of losses intensified Anne's grief.

> Sudden changes and simultaneous losses add extra dimension to your already difficult grief journey.

One major change has many other adjustments attached to it that you may not have considered. People do not necessarily realize the extra emotional turmoil that occurs when one loses the comfort of friends, the familiarity of one's home, and the stability of other connections. Related consequences may make a change less desirable, so do not forget to consider their effects.

Allow time to develop an accurate judgment rather than making hasty emotional decisions based on feelings. Emotions are manipulative deceivers, and can mislead us and distort our perceptions. Stay aware and be discerning when emotions and spiritual or personal decisions collide. Keeping emotions under control will help us stay on track with sound, measured reasoning.

THOUGHT TO WRITE ABOUT

In what way have emotions caused you to make bad decisions?

What are you doing to keep your emotions in check?

How are you handling decisions that are vulnerable to emotions?

Hope Thought:

Wrong input turns into wrong output. Are you feeding on lies or truth, trash or treasure, the world or the Word?

I've learned from experience that the greater part of our happiness or misery depends on our dispositions and not on our circumstances.

—Martha Washington

13

THOUGHTS ARE POWERFUL

I choose my thoughts. No thought, at any time, can
dwell in my mind without my permission.

—SHAD HELMSTETTER, PH.D.

When grief first engulfs us, we feel powerless—especially since we had no control over our loved one's life or death, and we were thrown into an inescapable circumstance because of it. However, each of us has the crucial task of guarding the doorways to our minds—and no one can do that for us.

Thoughts are critical. Satan's entrance into our lives is through our minds. Every sin begins with a thought, and many times, the thought seems fairly innocent or insignificant. However, a thought can grow and turn into an action that evolves into a pattern of negative behavior. Our thoughts can be friend or enemy. But *we* determine our thoughts.

Shad Helmstetter, in his revolutionary book, *What To Say When You Talk To Your Self,* discusses the importance of our thoughts:

We now know that by an incredibly complex physiological mechanism, a joint effort of body, brain and "mind," we become the living result of our own thoughts. Through scientific discovery we have proved the relationship between our own "mental programming" and the matter of whether we will succeed or fail in any endeavor we undertake in life, from something as important as a lifetime goal to something as small as what we do in a single day.

Additionally, our frames of mind determine much of what ultimately enters our lives. A positive attitude is a magnet for enthusiastic, hopeful people. Optimists attract and stimulate creative ideas and solutions, enabling them to face the world with more confidence and better coping skills.

Years ago, I had a dear friend named Kristen. One of the most positive people I have ever met, she always expected the best from everyone—and *expected* doors to open wide for her. She acted outside the box and confidently asserted that she was exempt from typical rules or constraints.

We attract what we project to others.

Consistently over time, I saw Kristen receive spontaneous favor in all types of situations. She would make a simple request and, instead, receive over and above what she had asked. People gave *generously* to her, whether material items, ideas, assistance, or whatever she needed.

In contrast, Kristen frequently traveled with a client (whose attitude was completely the opposite). Jim was critical, pessimistic, and anticipated the worst from people. Kristen told me about numerous incidents when they were together and strangers would approach Jim and say something negative, treat him harshly, argue with him for no apparent reason, or fail to assist him.

A different atmosphere surrounded these two people—and they attracted what they projected.

Do not give Satan the foothold he desires. If we leave him room to establish a footing, he will not stop until he acquires more territory. A steady pattern of negative thoughts counteracts healing. Instead, keeping an attitude of faithful expectation invites and enables God to work in your life.

By our attitudes, we prepare the "fertile soil" of our minds. So inevitably, we influence the outcome that grows out of our thoughts and the resulting actions. Our attitudes shape the character and substance of our lives. Helmstetter goes on to say:

> *Everything we do is affected directly or indirectly by our attitudes. A change in a person's attitude can affect just about everything else in that person's life. Our attitudes are our dispositions—they are the "state of mind" we live in. Our attitudes express themselves through our moods, our temperament, our willingness, and our hesitations . . . They are the foothold beneath us in every step we take . . . They are the single most determining factor in every action we will ever make. We and our attitudes are inextricably combined; we are our attitudes and our attitudes are us.*

> Our attitudes quite literally determine the direction and quality of our lives.

Echoing Helmstetter's words is a classic writing by Charles Swindoll from his book, *Strengthening Your Grip,* in which he, too, describes the power our attitudes hold over our lives:

ATTITUDES

Words can never adequately convey the incredible impact of our attitude toward life. The longer I live the more convinced I become that life is 10 percent what happens to us and 90 percent how we respond to it.

I believe the single most significant decision I can make on a day-to-day basis is my choice of attitude. It is more important than my past, my education, my bankroll, my successes or failures, fame or pain, what other people think of me or say about me, my circumstances, or my position. Attitude keeps me going or cripples my progress. It alone fuels my fire or assaults my hope. When my attitudes are right, there's no barrier too high, no valley too deep, no dream too extreme, no challenge too great for me.

I dreamed of being an interior designer from the time I was in junior high school. However, fear and practicality triumphed initially, and I earned a degree in business instead. After working in unfulfilling jobs for several years, I decided to go back to school and follow my dream. I was so excited and motivated that *nothing* would stand in my way this time.

The program was grueling beyond anything I expected, but I had a goal and I was determined to do my best. Obstacles developed—physical, mental, and relational—and stress intensified. However, I did not waver. Regardless of the time or effort required, I did what I needed to do. In fact, I graduated with a 4.0 average.

Attitude *is* powerful—and God honors our efforts when we honor Him with our best.

Attitudes Shape Our Thoughts

While our thoughts are always important because of the power of our minds, during times of great challenge like grief, our attitudes and thoughts are especially significant. All of us have encountered the downward spiral that occurs when we fail to control negative thinking. I have put myself into a tailspin too many times, and I am willing to bet you have done the same!

I hate to admit it, but I tend to ruminate. It's a good quality if you're pondering something positive, but with a negative, you can quickly tie yourself up in worry and despair. When I allowed myself to brood over what I had lost or fret over my future, nothing good came from it. In fact, I sank deeper into hopelessness.

By consciously rejecting my negative attitude and surrendering my thoughts and situation to God, things changed. *My attitude changed.*

> Focusing on the *possibilities* in an attitude
> of faith—activates doors we haven't even considered.

We have the ability to take an already difficult experience and make it even worse (or better) by how we approach it. We can choose to take upsetting situations and continually mull them over in our minds, but doing so only makes already tough circumstances even more devastating and challenging.

On the other hand, we can choose to face our situations with a constructive, optimistic attitude. The second option will yield clearer thinking and a better chance of reaching a rational solution with a positive outcome.

What we *believe* makes all the difference in the world.

We are more powerful than we sometimes *allow* ourselves to be. God gives us the power to make great changes in our lives—if we will change our expectations and our thoughts. If we continually think negative thoughts and expect to live a positive life, we will be disappointed.

Whether you believe you can do a thing or not, you are right.

—Henry Ford

But taking an offensive position—focusing on the *possibilities* in an attitude of faith—activates doors we haven't even considered. God says: . . . *"Forget about what's happened; don't keep going over old history. Be alert, be present. I'm about to do something brand-new. It's bursting out! Don't you see it? There it is! I'm making a road through the desert, rivers in the badlands."* (Isaiah 43:18–19, *MSG*)

Change Your Thoughts and You Can Change Your Life

In Joel Osteen's book, *Your Best Life Now Journal,* he discusses the potent effects our thoughts trigger:

> *Our thoughts contain tremendous power. Remember, we draw into our lives that which we constantly think about. If we're always dwelling on the negative, we will attract negative people, experiences, and attitudes. If we're always dwelling on our fears, we will draw in more fear. You are setting the direction of your life with your thoughts.*

You *get to choose* what you think about—either positive or negative. You do not have to ponder every thought that enters your mind. You can decide to change the negative thoughts into prayer, choose to dismiss them, or replace the negative with positive thoughts or beliefs.

Negative thoughts defeat us. They are Satan's accusers, causing doubt and disharmony. Along with widowhood came questioning thoughts that shook my confidence and self-esteem, such as: "You're forty-seven years old. How do you expect to meet anyone?" and, "Who is going to be interested in you? Men are attracted to younger women." These kinds of thoughts are destructive and will not only beat you down but *keep* you down if you allow them to persist.

So, constantly fight the battle to keep your mind focused in a good place.

Some people are able to rise above their circumstances while the very same things beat others down. The difference, in many cases, is how each person views her situation. *Perspective* makes a difference. What you *think* about your condition matters!

> *What's the difference between a stumbling block and a stepping stone? The way you approach it.*
> —Unknown Author

The Bible teaches us to guard our minds. God, in His wisdom, knows how powerful our thoughts are. They ultimately determine our lives . . . what we do and who we become. Our thoughts shape our characters and control our destinies—that is why they are so important:

> . . . fix your attention on God. You'll be changed from the inside out.
> Readily recognize what he wants from you, and quickly respond to it.
> Unlike the culture around you, always dragging you down to its level of immaturity,
> God brings the best out of you, develops well-formed maturity in you.
>
> —Romans 12:2–3 (*MSG*)

The Power of Positive Thinking

When we start to resist the negative and focus on the positive, fresh new attitudes begin to replace the old negative ones. When we trust God in the midst of our pain and problems, we open the door for His power to work in our lives.

God is not an intruder. He has given us free choice. So when we willfully refuse to ask for God's help and submit to His control, we miss out on His best for us—because God will not force Himself on us. While God is surely able to do anything He wishes in our lives, the Bible clearly says that without faith we cannot please Him.

For months, I refused to give God control over my relationships. I grew tired of waiting for someone to date and didn't see any hope of change, so I jumped in on my own. I seized control—and joined an online dating site, corresponded with the son of a family friend, and other activities as I sought companionship. *Everything* came to a dead end. Only when I submitted to God's control did things change.

God's plans (and His timing) do not usually make sense to us. While I was struggling to make something happen, the man whom I would eventually marry was not yet a widower. God has our best in mind, and I would have missed His best if I had kept control instead of relinquishing it to Him.

When we align ourselves with God's will, focus on His thoughts and promises, and submit to His commands, we activate His power and blessings in our lives. The Lord says:

> I will guide you along the pathway for your life.
> I will advise you and watch over you.
>
> —Psalm 32:8 (*NLT*)

Imagine God opening up the floodgates of Heaven and filling you with His goodness, power, and Grace to meet all your needs. When you align yourself with the will of God, you are inviting Him to work in your life. However, do not be deceived. You will have to make this decision time and again.

The battle for your mind continues all day, every day—because your mind is such a crucial battlefield. The winner of this battle controls your life. Be aware of what you are thinking.

We *can reprogram* our thinking by choosing not to dwell on the negative. When a negative thought enters your head, immediately reject it and replace it with something positive. Refocus.

> *The battle for your mind . . . is crucial. The winner controls your life.*

For example, a negative thought materializes: "Your best days are over. You will never be as happy as you were." As quickly as this thought forms, *reject* it. Counter the negative with a positive: "No! My days are bright, and God has good plans for me. Happiness is in my future." *Think about* the positive thoughts you just planted!

What we water, fertilize, and cultivate is what will grow. What we think about is what we draw to us. Our thoughts become self-fulfilling prophecies as our minds subconsciously work to execute our ideas.

For as he thinks in his heart, so is he.

—Proverbs 23:7 (*NKJV*)

As we focus on God's promises, faith and hope begin to flourish inside us. We begin to *expect* God's goodness and His power to work in our lives. We have opened the "faith" circuit that allows us to receive God's blessing. We have started to program success into our vocabulary. Osteen, in his book *Your Best Life Now*, shares this thought:

> *The only thing that limits God is your lack of faith . . . If you will put your trust in Him, God will make your life significant. God longs to make something great out of your life . . . But you must cooperate with God's plan; you must start thinking of yourself as the champion God made you to be.*

Keep the Faith and Affirm Your Beliefs

While significant loss is likely one of the most difficult conditions most people will face, grief does not have to be the end of the journey. Holding on to your faith means continuing to trust God even when you cannot see Him or feel His presence. Faith means trusting even when you do not feel like it.

Faith is not belief. Belief is passive. Faith is active.
—Edith Hamilton

Keeping your faith during a time of intense pain often requires fighting a raging internal battle. Faith moves you *to act*.

H. Norman Wright presents a creed in his book, *Experiencing Grief*, which affirms one's faith in God regardless of difficult circumstances or feelings. Wright advocates the value of affirming the creed daily, especially during the darkness of grief when keeping the faith feels like an insurmountable struggle:

> 'Believing against the grain' means having a survivalist attitude.
> Not only can we survive, but out of it we can create something good.
> We need to cry out, 'God help me believe!'

Affirmations create positive effects in people who apply them. Expressing your beliefs *aloud* will powerfully focus your thinking, and reminding yourself of God's presence in your life and in your pain will give you hope. Do not underestimate the authority of the spoken word. Following is the creed from Wright's book referred to above:

> *I believe God's promises are true.*
> *I believe heaven is real.*
> *I believe God will see me through.*
> *I believe nothing can separate us from God's love.*
> *I believe God has work for me to do.*

God will help us believe during this challenging time—we just need to ask. Sometimes keeping your faith and maintaining hope feels like a full-time job. And sometimes the task seems impossible.

Life as I had previously known it changed completely, and sometimes the myriad adjustments were unbearable. When discouragement took hold, I had to fight to keep hope alive. I prayed more than I ever had before, and I searched my Bible for specific promises to apply to my needs. I trusted in God's character and depended on His Word to carry me through.

God is waiting to help us. Everyone who seriously tries will find Him.

Maybe reading inspirational books helps you; or meditating on God's Word; listening to music; singing; praying; talking; walking in a peaceful, quiet setting; drawing or painting; or writing. Do whatever it takes!

Here is a comforting prayer of affirmation I wrote as a reminder of the power, presence, protection, and love of God. Carry it with you. Better yet, memorize the words so you can recall it when you need a faith-booster:

At the beginning of each day, I acknowledge,
with amazement and gratitude, that God is . . .
more than I can possibly imagine . . . and all I will ever need.
He is perfect and complete.

I have God's immeasurable love to nurture me;
God's strength to support me;
God's wisdom to direct me;
God's faithfulness to encourage and comfort me;
God's creativity to inspire me;
God's power to protect and enable me, and
God's Word to instruct me.
I have everything I need.

Thank you, God, for who you are!

God is waiting to help us. Everyone who seriously tries *will* find Him. Everyone can, if he really wants to.

God is in the business of rewriting our lives—and with the best possible plan in mind. His path is tested and foolproof.

God rewrote the text of my life when I opened the book of
    my heart to his eyes.
What a God! His road stretches straight and smooth.
Every God-direction is road-tested.
Everyone who runs toward him makes it.

—Psalm 18:24, 30 (*MSG*)

God Is Our Strength and Hope

Sometimes we do not know what to pray, or because of our states of mind, we don't have the capacity to pray; however, God promises to pray for us, *even when we cannot pray for ourselves:*

Meanwhile, the moment we get tired in the waiting, God's
  Spirit is right alongside helping us along.
If we don't know how or what to pray, it doesn't matter. He
  does our praying in and for us, making prayer out of
  our wordless sighs, our aching groans.
He knows us far better than we know ourselves, knows our
  pregnant condition, and keeps us present before God.
That's why we can be so sure that every detail in our lives of
  love for God is worked into something good.

—Romans 8:26–28 (*MSG*)

God's Word does not change—and is the *one thing* in this
world we can count on completely.

Hold on to His truth, meditate on it, let it *bloom* in your heart,
and depend on God to carry you through this dark time to the light
beyond.

There were times when my grief was so agonizing, I could not
pray. I was unable to say anything—and all I could do was cry. How
phenomenal to know that God's Spirit was interceding for me, doing
what I could not do for myself. What a reassuring, mind-boggling
promise from God!

Keep reminding yourself that the pain will not last forever . . . the
pain will not last forever . . . the pain will not last forever.

THOUGHT TO WRITE ABOUT

Make a list of your greatest blessings. For whom and for what do you thank God the most?

Hope Thought:

I'm not qualified to run the universe—but God is!

Miracles don't happen until we step out and risk—Peter had to get out of the boat before he could walk on water. When God shows up—*things happen.*

> *Pain becomes bearable when we are able to trust that it won't last forever, not when we pretend that it doesn't exist.*
>
> —ALLA BOZARTH-CAMPBELL
> (FROM *Life Is Goodbye/Life Is Hello*)

PART

TWO

REMAPPING MY LIFE

Where Do I Go from Here?

14

ACKNOWLEDGING YOUR
LOSS IS CRUCIAL TO HEALING

Grief

Always toward its destiny,
Grief, like a river, flows through my life,
Its journey never ending.
Sometimes flowing smoothly, gliding,
My memories are at peace.
Then comes a raging flood,
As sorrow tears my soul apart.
Always the flood subsides.
The river flows smoothly.
Life goes on toward eternity.
For a while grief sits in the corner of my heart
And watches the river flow by.

—JANIS M. BRIZENDINE

Facing your loss directly, and eventually being willing (and able) to accept the loss, are essential to healing. Understand that carrying out this step does not happen all at once, but little by little. The process is *gradual*—and slowly evolves as you are able to cope with your questions and emotions.

As we have learned, talking about your loss helps you accept it. In addition, when you do the short exercises in this book and respond to the journaling questions, you will be facing your feelings and working through your grief. These activities are invaluable to your healing. Do not hastily dismiss them or discount their worth.

In the grief-support workshops, one exercise consisted of drawing a picture of our broken hearts and talking about what we had lost. The exercise is effective. My illustration consisted of an empty white heart, split in two by way of rough, jagged edges at its center, and surrounded by a black box.

Remapping Exercise: Drawing of My Broken Heart

My drawing signified the pain and emptiness I felt after John's death. The rough, jagged edges down the center of the heart represented how his death fiercely ripped apart and wounded my own heart. The disconnected sections of the heart symbolized how the reality of death had physically separated the two of us. The encompassing black box illustrated my feeling that grief had abruptly dumped me into a bleak, scary, bottomless crater of pain where I was slowly drowning. The plain white heart symbolized the emptiness that fully engulfed me because of my husband's death.

My heart felt like an empty, lifeless shell, stripped of its joy, color, and vitality.

Excerpt from My Personal Journal (1999) about "What has been lost . . ."

- *A mate to share all of life's experiences*
- *A mate whose differences brought richness to our relationship, whose strengths complemented my weaknesses and vice versa*
- *Someone who loved me above all others*

- *My best friend with whom I could share anything and everything*
- *My lover*
- *My biggest cheerleader*
- *My traveling companion*
- *My physical fitness "conscience"*
- *A partner to share responsibilities and help make decisions*
- *A mate who, with his help, moved me to do things I wouldn't have done on my own*
- *Someone with the most joyous spirit, greatest sense of adventure, and zest for living I've ever known*
- *The person I was closest to in the world*
- *A house filled with laughter and someone to come home to*

While this exercise and the journal writing may seem silly and pointless, their effects have been powerful among grief-group participants. These activities force you to come face to face with the death or other loss—and thoughtfully consider what this reality means. Completing the exercises draws out emotions that are crucial to work through, and confronting them brings healing.

Another benefit of the drawing exercise is to help someone close to you understand your loss. Sharing with others lessens the pain and brings people together. Paula, a middle-aged widow, showed her drawing to her adult son and explained its meaning to him. While they already had a close relationship and frequently spent time together, he did not understand how much his mom was struggling or how she really felt. Reviewing her exercise with him created an opportunity for the two of them to talk about their mutual loss, and the insights both of them gained from each other strengthened their bond.

Face Grief to Find Peace

Grief is an undeniable part of life. And bits and pieces of grief will always stay with us . . . memories triggered by words, songs, photos, places, other people, and thoughts—so many different reminders. In time, however, the onslaught of emotions will no longer be a raging flood, nor will the grief be all-encompassing. You *can* come to terms with grief and be at peace.

What Does "Healing from Grief" Mean?

Healing from grief is not the same as healing from an illness or disease. The remnants of grief *do not permanently disappear* when healing occurs.

Typically, when medical treatment successfully cures a physical disease the symptoms go away. But grief operates differently. With grief, residual effects linger for years, or for the rest of your life; however, do not let this statement frighten you.

Your loss can suddenly trigger emotions and reactions—and these potential responses will be with you always. But over time, they can turn into tender, precious, positive reminders instead of painful ones.

> You'll grow accustomed to the ebb and flow of your own grief, which isn't a negative, even though it may sound that way right now. After a while, you accept the ever-present, just-below-the-surface marks of love.

Sometimes tears crop up unexpectedly, and I have learned to accept them without embarrassment. Five or six years after my husband died, I was having a conversation with a leader at church. She asked me what had happened to him, and as I told her the story, I could hardly utter the words between the tears. Over the years, I had been asked this question many times, and my response was not always so emotional. Why then? I have no explanation. However, I am grateful that my heart is filled with love and not bitterness—and thankful for memories that are still sweet.

> *Grief is like a disability—you don't get over it, you just learn to live with it.*
> *—Val Secarea (grief traveler)*

Healing from grief means you have faced your loss; experienced the resulting pain; released your loved one and your loss; and you are now directing your energies toward remapping your life into a satisfying one without the presence of your loved one.

Healing does not mean all evidence of grief is gone and renewal is complete. Healing does not mean your pain will instantly disappear. Healing does not mean you will suddenly be happy again—or you will not continue to experience trials and adjustments as you develop your new "normal."

Healing does mean your pain will be less intense and less frequent. In addition, healing also means you have redirected your energy from the past, and from dealing primarily with your loss, in order to refocus your strength toward creating a new life.

Healing from grief is a little confusing at first because of its erratic nature. This quality makes the process difficult to track and muddles your perception of progress.

But once you understand how healing works, you can adjust your thinking. Unexpected surprises can cause setbacks and disappointment, so knowing what to expect prepares you to keep moving toward restoration, renewal, and a "new normal."

THOUGHT TO WRITE ABOUT

Draw a picture of your broken heart.

Describe the elements of your picture and what you have lost, and share this exercise with a close friend or family member.

Hope Thought:

I take myself too seriously and I don't take God seriously enough.

I need to refocus. Adjust my thinking. And block out the distracting interference.

The first rule of focus is this: "Wherever you are, be there."

—ANONYMOUS

15

. . . .

RELEASE:
ENDINGS AND BEGINNINGS

. . . .

When we come close to those things that break us
down, we touch those things that also break us open.

—WAYNE MULLER

Release

You will finally reach the time when you must release your grief and release your loved one. However, you will likely reach this point slowly, perhaps very slowly. Each person's timetable is different. For months (or even years in some cases), grievers navigate the everyday responsibilities of living, but carry on halfheartedly much of the time. They go through the motions, do what they must do, but live without passion. It is like living life on *autopilot.*

A moment will happen—and many remember the specific turning point—when they made the decision to live again. *Really live!* Making the decision to re-engage fully in life is a major milestone. However, release will not happen immediately and completely—it is a process.

Release does not mean forgetting. Sometimes people are genuinely afraid of forgetting their loved ones, and they confuse release with forgetting. We could never forget persons or relationships that were so important and such a part of us, so don't worry needlessly about forgetting.

The key to release is not forgetting, but choosing to live again.

With release, we begin to divert the energy we invested in our grief and instead, devote it toward embracing a new life. The focus shifts from death, loss, and grief to renewed life and its related transitions. Memories start to bring gentle smiles instead of painful tears.

The key to release is not forgetting, but choosing to live again.

> My life was suddenly divided into before and after;
> and there was no going back to before.
> But then I realized I had a choice to live the after.
> I had to decide.
> —Brenda Neal

Preserving Memories

To release the "fear of forgetting," you may want to assemble a tangible remembrance of your loved one that consists of items meaningful to you.

I created a special book for Kelly that celebrates her dad's life. I pored through loads of favorite photos of John and our family and selected the best ones for the album. I also included the memorial booklet she and I designed for the service when we scattered John's ashes. After he died, I received countless cards and letters, many of them from people I had never met, telling me about heartwarming encounters they had had with John. Coworkers wrote about times when he had made a difference in their lives, or when he had shared loving words or stories with them about Kelly or me. These cherished keepsakes, an irreplaceable link to John, were too important to lose—so I put them in our memory book. Kelly was barely twenty-eight when her dad died, so these symbols of his life will always remind her of the special man he was.

> *The soul would have no rainbows had the eyes no tears.*
>
> —*John Vance Cheney*

Various people I know have safeguarded their memories in other ways. Several have had framed shadow boxes made that contain important mementos of their loved ones. A young woman who lost her mom took a beautiful box, and inside the box, she placed all sorts of articles that convey precious memories of her mother . . . such as handwritten notes from her mom, a journal, a gold locket, photos, a familiar handkerchief, a memorial booklet, and her mom's bible. This box is a treasure to her—and a way to share her mother with others, even people who never met her. The process of putting such a remembrance together is a step toward healing.

You will face your grief and experience the emotions that go along with it as you remember—and, at the same time, you will be preserving valuable memories.

Surrender to God's Plan

For a believer, release also means surrendering your new future to God, *whatever* He has in store for you. After John's death, I struggled with God and myself over my circumstances. I knew I did not want to be alone for the rest of my life. Everything seemed to be at a stand-still. And there was *no hint* of any change about to take place or in the future. (Of course, God's timing and ours *rarely* coincide.)

A tug-of-war took center stage inside of me. I was not satisfied with my life, I did not want to be alone, and yet I wanted to trust God and follow Him. Back and forth we went. I literally had to reach a place of accepting God's will for my future, whatever He decided, regardless of my own ideas. I had to relax and be at peace with where I was.

I gave up the battle because I realized the details were not in my hands. And I stopped trying to control everything myself. I prayed and reminded God (as though He needed reminding!) of my dreams, but told Him I accepted whatever He planned for me. Then I lived my life as fully as possible. I pursued activities I enjoyed, spent time with family and friends, took seminars, read, and went places on my own. I *embraced* my life as best I could. My hope for a mate was still tucked away in my mind, but I stopped trying to force something to happen.

Finally, I was able to take the step and trust God. This part of release is critical. As a Christian, I was living outside of God's will by not surrendering. To my surprise, things began to change once I stopped struggling and yielded control to God.

Journaling Brings Release

The act of release is a powerful turning point in your grief journey.

Journaling enables you to confront feelings, thoughts, or barriers, and then experience and release them. Journaling is an *active, concrete* activity. The action of release may mean writing a series of entries and re-reading them until you can embrace and act upon what you have written. Who, or what, do you need to release?

The following is a journal entry I wrote in 1999, a "Letter of Release" to my husband:

Dear John,

I can't think about you without smiling and remembering the wonderful times we shared—remembering your laughter and your total joy in living. How excited you got about the simplest things! How much I miss my best friend and the quiet, away times we spent together as well as special times with family and friends. How you entertained all of us with your stories and your infectious laugh!

But then my mind always returns to the last Saturday you were alive. I wish I had stayed home that day; that I had gone to the store with you that morning; that we had spent time together talking and laughing; that I had said something memorable before I left; that we could just go back and relive that day and recapture those moments.

I wish we had known to check further into the condition of your heart. If we had just known something was wrong. And I keep asking— "Why didn't the doctors know?"

I realize there are no answers and I have to let go, but it's so hard when all I want to do is bring you back. We used to talk often about how lucky we were to have each other and to have been married for so long—how we wanted to grow old together, and how we looked forward to the time when we could travel and spend more time with each other. Unfortunately, our plans were not God's plans.

If one of us had to go first, I'm thankful it was you because I love you too much to see you go through this pain. And knowing you the way I do, as difficult as this grief is for me, I know it would have been worse for you.

I love you with all my heart and I always will. We were different in so many ways, but I loved that about you. I look at our sweet daughter and I see you because she is so much like you. You'd be so proud of her! She has been a lifeline to me since you died. Without her, I don't think I could have gone on. We have supported each other, and the closeness we've always shared has become even more strong and tender.

Last night I sobbed as I prayed. It was hard, but I gave you back to the Lord. You aren't mine to hold onto any longer. I have to keep reminding myself that the Lord took you home. That's where you belong now, and I have to begin to let go. You will always be in my heart and that will never change, but I have to let go.

I know you are in God's care and so are we—I just have to remind myself each day.

When I see a star in the sky or the wind blowing, I like to think you are there—no longer bound by space or time, experiencing the adventures you always craved. So for now, you'll just have to experience the joy for both of us—and share your exciting stories with me when we meet again.

All my love,
Judy

The act of release is a powerful turning point in your grief journey. This significant step signaled a change in my thinking. I was accepting the unchangeable reality of my husband's death and starting to let go of the past. I was acknowledging the truth about my own life because of his death. And if I were ever going to build a fulfilling life again, I had to look to the future.

New Beginnings

Melissa, a hopeful and determined widow I met through a grief workshop, told me about a saying her daughter shared with her many years earlier when she was going through a difficult time. Her daughter said, "*Don't look back; you are not going that way.*" This saying brought her strength years ago, and she now relies on these words throughout the day. Her daughter's reassuring words are a positive reminder of release and new beginnings.

> "*Don't look back, you are not going that way.*"
> —*Author Unknown*

Melissa also wrote, "*Life is moving and I must work through the grieving. I do not want to become stagnant and wallow in my sorrow. That is not productive for anyone.*"

Remind yourself to keep looking forward because that's the way you're headed. Forward, not backward.

Release: Endings Become New Beginnings

The force of life is stronger than death. Life calls. Hope calls. Sunshine calls.

Will you answer?

Endings become new beginnings. Releasing the past, embracing new beginnings . . . may seem completely impossible. But remember, nothing is impossible with God . . . even new beginnings.

THOUGHT TO WRITE ABOUT

Describe ways in which you are beginning to release your loved one or your loss.

How will you preserve special memories?

Hope Thought:

Whenever you feel weak, God is reminding you to depend on Him. You may be weak . . . but He isn't.

> *The past was a nice place to visit. But it is not a good place to live.*
> *Now a door is opened.*
> *And streaming through the doorway is the bright sunshine of the future.*
>
> —HAL LARSON & SUSAN LARSON
> (FROM *Suddenly Single*)

16

....

"REMAPPING" YOUR LIFE

....

Although the world is full of suffering, it is also full of the overcoming of it.

—HELEN KELLER

What Is Remapping?

Remapping is a descriptive term coined to illustrate the entire process of moving full-circle from loss to expectantly living again. The word made an indelible impression on me when I first heard it expressed, just in passing, during a grief-support workshop. In attempting to describe changes and challenges he faced after the death of his wife, a widower intuitively labeled the recovery process *remapping*. The word paints a perfect picture of what happens when someone resolves loss in a healthy way.

> Remapping does not consist of a canned, predictable, systematic checklist.

When you lose someone or something vital to your life, you run into abrupt dead-ends in place of certain roads and bridges you had before . . . paths that now stop suddenly and lead nowhere.

The roads you traveled before your loss were filled with familiar signs, shared experiences and associations, common interests and attachments, comfortable ways of thinking and relating to others, plans, and dreams. These 'roads' were a basic part of who you were and how you communicated—and they *led somewhere.* They connected you to your loved one and your world.

Your loss, however, changed the old roads forever. You can no longer reach your destination the former ways because some of them are either impassable or altogether gone. Severed connections need to be replaced with new ones.

In God's master plan, constant change is the norm, and this life cycle is as true for nature as it is for people. Beginnings turn into endings that lead to new beginnings. Since this cycle of life/death/ constant change/and loss is a natural, inescapable part of our lives, well-being and happiness depend upon learning how to accept and cope with it.

What Do I Have to Do?

Remapping does not consist of a canned, predictable, systematic checklist directing you from Point A to Point B and so on. Instead, remapping is a process unique to each individual.

> Remapping is a personal process of pain and sadness, acceptance, release, discovery, healing, and renewal unique to each individual, as distinct as each person's own life and loss.

We have been talking about aspects of remapping throughout this book as we've discussed every topic. Confronting each of the important grief issues is a step in the remapping process. So let's just talk about it more specifically here.

Some basic elements remain constant, regardless of your own path or timetable, or the grief issue you are dealing with at any given moment. Remember, remapping is a *process*, not an event. And these key components can be seen as an overall framework to keep in mind as you go through the remapping actions we'll discuss a little later.

First, you have to take the **time**—because remapping happens over time, not immediately or in a single step. Another principle relates to your **feelings**. To heal from the pain, you have to allow yourself to feel the emotions. Eventually, you will be able to **accept** your new reality and **release** your loved one and your loss. In time, as healing progresses, you **reopen your heart** to fully live and love again. Finally, remember that remapping is not a Lone Ranger process—you do not want to try to do this all by yourself. You need **support**.

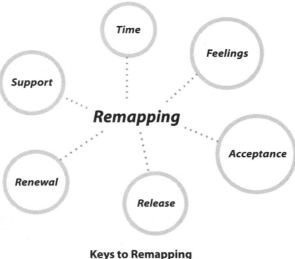

Keys to Remapping

What Does God Say about It?

Remapping is a new way of looking at grief . . . which is a process of resolution and renewal. God designed grieving to enable us to handle our inevitable losses. While you may not think grieving *feels* normal, it is a normal process. It is what we need to do to reach a point where we can let go of someone (or something) we no longer have. Only by going full circle *through* the grief, or remapping, can we let go of our pain and wholly open ourselves up to new life.

> Out of every crisis comes the choice to be reborn . . .
> to choose the kind of change that will help us to
> grow and fulfill ourselves more completely.
> —Nena O'Neill

Do not let the prospect of remapping frighten or overpower you. Just begin. And don't try to be stubbornly independent and do it alone.

The Bible is clear that God did not create us to grieve alone, but in community. God comforts us so we *can comfort* others (II Cor. 1:3–7). He tells us to *share in the sorrow* of others as well as in their happiness (Rom. 12:15). The Bible is filled with references to tears, sorrow, grieving, mourning, weeping, comforting . . . and yet for some reason, we are uneasy (and sometimes ashamed) to outwardly show our pain or let anyone know we are trying to work through our losses.

Does our discomfort about grief make sense? God *designed us* to grieve so we can experience the good awaiting us on the other side of loss. *He wired us* to grieve.

Remapping—a Process of Restoration

Thinking of remapping as a process of restoration will begin to change a misguided mindset that views grieving as a negative. Remapping is positive and healthy. It represents growth, learning, and change.

If we have a community of support, even one person who is there for us, we do not have to panic about the void left by our losses because we do not have to face them alone. Please do not try to do this by yourself. You need support.

Remapping Actions

Here are a few remapping actions, and we will talk about others as we go along. (You will notice some repetition, but bear with me—these actions are key.)

- Think about and candidly face what has happened along with your questions and emotions
- *Feel* your feelings
- Talk and write about what is on your mind and heart
- Begin to replace shattered connections with new ones
- Slowly, as you ease back into life, allow your heart to reopen
- Keep going until you have gone full-circle—you'll know when you get there because the old wounds will not feel the same as before
- Take one step at a time
- Don't think too far ahead

Expect to go through setbacks, but that is okay. Setbacks are normal.

> Remember the jagged path of grief—forward and backward steps, ups and downs . . . not a straight, continuous path.

After being a widow for two-and-a-half years, I thought I was finally ready to date. I was nervous, but cautiously excited about moving ahead with my life; however, I was shocked to quickly find out I was mistaken.

I knew Ted casually through work. We had talked with ease on the phone many times and been in meetings together, so I did not think going out with him would be *too* intimidating. We arranged to go to a basketball game, and he picked me up at work so we could get there in time. I felt a bit awkward, but after all, this was my first date in nearly thirty years!

We headed off to the game (seemed safe enough) so I tried to settle down, get to know Ted a little better, and enjoy the evening. We had to travel more than an hour to reach the game site, leaving us *a whole lot* of time in the car to talk. The pressure was on . . . and it took its toll. I'm not exactly a freewheeling small talker!

Truthfully, the date wigged me out a little, and memories of my husband flooded my mind. As the night wore on, I recognized I should not be there. Everything I did or said felt uncomfortable, but I hoped Ted didn't notice. I tried to enjoy the rest of the evening, but was unnerved and anxious for the date to end. When he dropped me off after the game, I still had to drive home. I couldn't wait to escape to the "sanctuary" of my car, and I cried all the way home, upset and discouraged. I think I cried myself to sleep, too.

I was *not* emotionally ready to take the dating step, so I backed up and waited another six months or so before trying again. Then I knew the time was right to move forward.

You will experience setbacks and everything will not be smooth sailing, but just keep going down the path. It *will* be all right.

Unresolved grief does not eventually disappear or resolve itself.

You can't lead a healthy, happy life if you are unable to fully grieve your losses. The alternative is tragically sad.

I recently met a middle-aged man named Joe whose wife died more than thirty years ago. He has two children, a daughter, Julie, and a son named Mike. The kids were eight and ten years old when an emergency forced Joe to rush his wife, Susan, to the hospital. Julie rode in the car with her dad during the traumatic ride. Mike was staying at his cousin's house for a sleepover. Complications arose and Susan died.

Unresolved loss. More than thirty years have passed, and Joe has been unable to sustain a relationship with another woman. He has battled severe health problems, including cancer and diabetes, and has undergone chemotherapy and major surgeries. Mike wrestled for years with an overpowering sense of guilt because he was absent when his mom died. The crisis Julie witnessed on the way to the hospital devastated her, leaving permanent marks. And both children have struggled with substance abuse plus emotional, relational, and career problems their entire lives.

Each of these people failed to remap their losses, and the resulting brokenness prevented them from leading emotionally healthy, satisfied lives from then on.

Unresolved grief does not eventually disappear or resolve itself. The value of remapping is so great you cannot put a price on it. We're talking about your life. *Your extraordinary life.*

> I think these difficult times have helped me to understand better than before how infinitely rich and beautiful life is in every way . . .
> —Isak Dinesen

Don't let *anything* get in your way. Run the whole race, go full circle, and trust the remapping process.

You have only one life. Rekindle your passion, and don't allow unresolved grief to snatch your life away. Glade Byron Addams captured the essence of what I'm trying to convey when he said, "*Chase down your passion like it's the last bus of the night.*" What a visual!

Life is all about passion. So run for your life!

What steps you are taking to remap your life?

THOUGHT TO WRITE ABOUT

- Replacing severed connections?

- Journaling to work through issues and feelings?

- Talking about what happened?

- *Allowing* yourself to enjoy life again?

Where are you on the remapping "circle"?

Hope Thought:

Start dreaming a dream. You have something to offer the world that no one else has.

Think about it. Picture it. *Take a step.*

> *If you don't know where you're going, you'll end up somewhere else.*
>
> —ALFRED ADLER

17

....

REMAPPING 101:
WILL YOU TAKE THE RISK?

....

One of the secrets of life is to make stepping stones out of stumbling blocks.

—Unknown Author

Oue of grief's greatest stumbling blocks, especially among widows and widowers, is having no idea how to reconfigure their lives without their partners. Many issues affect a person's difficulty in making the transition, such as: the griever's age (and possibly gender), depth of the couple's relationship, length of their marriage, extent of social contacts, personality of the griever, quality of the support system, and other personal factors.

> *Remapping does not happen unconsciously or without focused energy.*

Most people have absolutely *no idea* how or where to start remapping their lives. A widower in a grief-support group compared his loss and the process of putting one's life back together again to digging a huge hole in the front yard with a back-hoe and tediously filling it back in with a teaspoon. Grief attacks suddenly and completely after the death occurs—while the process of recovery and restoration is slow and, at times, seemingly endless and insurmountable.

Remapping Your Life

Remapping does not happen unconsciously or without focused energy. Creating a new and satisfying life takes effort, perseverance, determination, and even imagination. It also takes a willingness to experiment, fail, and then try something different.

Most of us settle into our lifestyles and become comfortable, even complacent. When an unforeseen event changes the course and substance of our lives, we're unsure how to blaze a trail or set a new direction.

Success is not final, failure is not fatal: it is the courage to continue that counts.
—Sir Winston Churchill

Where do we start? What do we do? Can we make it happen? Will we be happy again?

Is the effort worth it?

Keeping an open mind is essential during this rebuilding process. Having a willingness to experiment and fail is even more important. And maintaining an attitude of "not taking yourself too seriously" will help.

Most of us are overly self-conscious and sensitive as we begin to test these untested waters. We feel as if everyone is looking at us as though we have purple hair or we are the elephant in the middle of the room.

Stressful? Unsettling? Intimidating?

Definitely . . . but not impossible.

What Can You Do?

As a widow, I was undeniably lost socially. Apart from my married friends and my daughter, I was alone. My social life was totally linked with my husband's, and I did not have any single friends. Most of my family lived thousands of miles away. My work was consuming and somewhat isolating, and my job provided few prospects for meeting singles.

My connections through outside activities or organizations were limited, so as a single person, I noticed few social prospects. I had to get creative about figuring out how an almost fifty-ish, single woman could start from scratch and develop a satisfying social life when *nothing* was obvious to me.

Fear and anxiety immobilize you, and immobility breeds lifelessness . . . so one of the first steps in remapping is to *take action*. As with many other things, the first step is usually the hardest.

The key is to start *somewhere!*

Even though you may want to move forward in your life, you may have one foot on the brakes. In order to be free, we must learn to let go . . .

—Mary Manin Morrissey

Step Out and Try Something New

You can test the waters at home, if you wish, which may be the most comfortable and least intimidating place to start trying new things.

Look around.

Maybe a long time has passed since you have made any changes in your living environment. Perhaps a little change inside your home would lift your spirits or vary your outlook. Try cleaning or organizing a space, painting a room a different color, adding some new pillows to your living room, choosing new linens for your bed, or purchasing a piece of art. What about planting some flowers or buying some plants for inside your house?

The idea is to do something that will create freshness and a sense of optimism in the space where you live every day.

> While superficial changes may seem trivial, as I tried new
> things and made small changes . . .
> I started to think differently.

Possibly, you'll want to start even closer to home—on yourself. Maybe a few additions to your wardrobe or a little change in the way you dress will change your attitude. I remember thinking I needed a new look. I had worn the same hairdo for a long time, so I decided to change my style and experiment with physical training. I joined a gym (a first for me!) and began a regular workout program. As I started to get in shape and lose a few pounds I felt better, and, surprisingly, my confidence slowly returned. The first time someone said to me, "*You work out, don't you?*" was a *wow* moment!

The self is not something ready-made, but something in continuous formation through choice of action.
—John Dewey

While these superficial changes may seem trivial, as I tried new things and made small changes, I felt more powerful. I started to think differently. I also became more certain I would be able to make other needed adjustments, perhaps even the uncomfortable ones.

Attitude is a determining factor in how we see our world and face our circumstances, and in how we feel. We're facing a new chapter in life, so we might as well try to make it as pleasant as possible. In some ways, it may even be exciting.

Changes are scary, but they can also be energizing. Approaching the changes with optimism and an open mind will make the transition easier—and certainly more pleasant.

Get Creative and Think Outside Your Box

What do you like? Maybe there's somewhere you have longed to go, or something you have always wanted to see, do, or learn—but just never had the time or opportunity. *Now* is the time.

Take advantage of the chance to do something for yourself. For pure fun or for the mental challenge, here are some ideas:

- Take a class
- Read a book
- Learn a craft, e.g., jewelry-making, knitting, needle-point, scrapbooking
- Experiment with photography
- Go to the theater
- Take a train trip or a cruise
- Learn to sew
- Volunteer and make a difference in someone else's life
- Visit friends
- Go away for the weekend
- Go to a movie or try a new restaurant

- Buy concert tickets
- Visit a museum or art gallery
- Try sculpture or painting
- Take a trip overseas or somewhere you've never been
- Go hiking
- Try skydiving
- Take dance lessons
- Join an aerobics or Pilates class
- Sign up for a reading group
- Join some interesting organizations
- See what you can come up with to add to the list!

Do something new. Start a fun "to do" list and add to it whenever you get an idea—and then start trying the things on your list. Come up with as many ideas as you can. Make this a happy, creative exercise—and think outside of your typical box. It's best to make a note of ideas *as they come to mind* or you may forget.

I loved reading Dr. Seuss books to Kelly when she was young, so when I ran across his quotation below, I had to smile. It really is amazing what we can do when we are open to new ideas.

> Think left and think right and think low and think high. Oh,
> the thinks you can think up if only you try!
> —Dr. Seuss

You Can Go Alone!

You may be thinking—"Fine, but with whom do I do these things?"

You are able to do many things alone. At first, I didn't feel comfortable going out to dinner or to a movie alone. *But I did it anyway!* I was not going to let the fact that I was alone stop me from doing things I enjoyed. Besides, the nice thing about going alone was that I could decide at the last moment to go—and just go.

> *Seeing yourself as you want to be is the key to personal growth.*
> *—Unknown Author*

If you feel uncomfortable sitting alone in a restaurant, take a book or magazine with you and read while you eat, or work a Sudoku or crossword puzzle. Having a prop actually does help relieve the discomfort of feeling conspicuous and not quite knowing what to do with yourself while eating alone, at least at first.

Start picturing yourself enjoying a night out as you dine alone in a pleasant setting. To forget about your uneasiness, focus on whatever you are doing—the food, the atmosphere, the magazine you brought, and other people.

If entering a movie theater alone makes you feel obvious, take your seat once the lights go down. After doing this a couple of times, your initial resistance starts fading—and the freedom takes over. It is liberating.

If you enjoy traveling, but the thought of touring solo is too scary, boring, or simply unappealing, consider going on an escorted tour. Many fine ones are available, and they eliminate much of the guesswork and preparation connected with travel. You can select a tour based on the level of planning you want, i.e., trips with or without air transportation and transfers in addition to lodging, ground transportation, number of meals, special events, outings and side trips, and so on. When you purchase a package, the tour company handles essential details for you.

Wide varieties of tours are available. Some options are:

- Adventure travel

- Solo travel

- Gender-specific trips

- Educational excursions

- Cultural experiences

- Nature tours

- Culinary and gourmet trips

- Senior tours

- Luxury trips

- Budget travel

- Shopping expeditions

- Golfing vacations

- Historical trips

- Holiday tours

- Religious tours

- Inland waterway excursions

- And more (check it out!)

You can feel more secure about the safety and companionship of traveling with others. Even on highly planned trips, you still have blocks of free time to spend as you wish. Group travel can be an exciting, fun alternative to going solo.

A trip will get you out of the house and give you something to anticipate. Check into the multitude of available options, plan something, and pencil in a date on your calendar!

Focus on Being Positive, Approachable, and Powerful

Begin to look for opportunities to invite new people into your life.

Join organizations, introduce yourself to people you come into contact with, and become more accessible, even outwardly friendly, to those you may not have approached before. Typically, you may not have thought to invite someone to coffee or brunch, or offer to carpool with a colleague, or invite an acquaintance to an art gallery opening or lecture, or initiate an outing with someone you just recently met. Don't wait. Make the first move.

> Start looking at your new freedom as a positive possibility instead of a perpetual prison.

Try some things you would not normally do.

One of my married friends told me about a single woman she and her husband had met on numerous occasions while walking their dogs. They found out she was starting a small group (from our church) in her home, thought we would like each other, and suggested that I contact her and go to the group. Since I had no single friends, I thought, "Why not?" So I went. What a great decision that was! Abby and I discovered we had interests in common—and we shared many enjoyable times. We went to movies, art galleries, out to dinner, to concerts, and to church together. I was glad I said *yes* to the opportunity.

Start to think in new ways. Talk to people. Ask questions that require more than a "yes" or "no" answer so you can get to know new acquaintances. Take a few chances.

Impossible is only in the dictionary of fools.

—Napoleon Bonaparte

Eliminate powerless words from your vocabulary—words such as *can't, maybe, unlikely, or should*. Focus on positive and powerful declarations: *I can, I will, and I do*. Focus on God and His unlimited power. I once heard a pastor say, *"God's vocabulary does not contain the word 'impossible'—so neither should ours!"* He went so far as to remove this word from his dictionary.

Start looking at your new freedom as a positive possibility instead of a perpetual prison. Get in touch with your creative energy. Each of us is creative in some way—so embrace your creativity.

A time will come when you can actually enjoy solitude again, and solitary activities can be peaceful, relaxing, and revitalizing. Do not let your thinking confine you. Be open to new options.

Jane is an extrovert and loves the energy and excitement of being around people. After her divorce, she realized she could barely stand to be alone in her home. The emptiness and quiet drove her crazy—and left her with *too much* time alone.

Don't be afraid to try something out of character or unexpected.

She needed solitude to work through her feelings, but she also wanted to recapture the joy of being at home. Secretly, Jane had a desire to paint. So she purchased a canvas and art supplies—and started dabbling. Painting simultaneously relaxed and energized her, and she lost all track of time as she explored a new creative outlet. This "experiment" changed Jane's outlook—and she no longer avoided being home. Don't be afraid to try something out of character or unexpected.

Be courageous enough to step into the light—whatever that *step forward* represents to you. Let go of whatever is holding you back.

Don't Give In—It's Not Easy, but You Can Do It

Many times during this trial-and-error remapping, you will be tempted to feel sorry for yourself or to give in to a defeatist or victim mentality. Practice replacing those thoughts with positive, powerful ones. This process is not effortless. But it is definitely doable. It can even be inspiring.

For more than a year after my husband died, I had no desire to develop a social life. The grief was too raw. However, once I did reach that point, I was stuck. My first thought was, "This is *never* going to work. I don't even know where to start." But I didn't allow myself the luxury of comfortably staying there. I started a workout program at the gym, and then realized I could do other things I had not done before. One victory planted the idea of others. I was motivated!

> Victories, even small ones, can trigger a powerful momentum. Success sparks joy, ignites imagination, and draws you back into life.

You will feel a sense of satisfaction and strength growing inside that reminds you of how far you have come. Appreciate the personal growth you have accomplished because of the unwanted road you've traveled. You can do this.

You gain strength, courage and confidence by every experience in which you really stop to look fear in the face.

You are able to say to yourself, "I have lived through this
    horror. I can take the next thing that comes along" . . .
You must do the thing you think you cannot do.

—Eleanor Roosevelt

I believe with all my heart that the grief journey can be a positively defining, life-changing experience. True, your life will never be the same. But how you allow grief to affect your life is your choice.

Loss Can Teach Us Valuable Lessons

In his book, *Awakening from Grief,* John Welshons writes about the lessons we can learn from loss:

> *Suffice it to say that I now know that death and loss can be our greatest teachers. They're our greatest teachers because, in tearing away the people, possessions, the hopes and dreams we all cling to, they offer us the opportunity to find out who we really are, to discover the depths of our beings . . .*

In time, grief can be the beginning of . . .
. . . new self-confidence
. . . new priorities
. . . new friendships and richer relationships
. . . greater compassion for others
. . . a deeper appreciation for life

Farther down the road, as *you* change—your journey through
    loss may lead to . . .
. . . setting and working toward new goals
. . . reexamining your life purpose

. . . truly grasping the irreplaceable value of time

. . . facing and accepting death, thus learning to *really* live

. . . a closer walk with God

In *Awakening from Grief,* Welshons goes on to discuss the positive effects that are possible as a result of grief:

> *Our grief can be our undoing. It can turn us off to ourselves—to our lives and to our world. Or . . . it can be the sword that tears our hearts open, that allows us to be vulnerable, that takes away our illusion of control, our self-imposed distance from our capacity to love and surrender. If we can meet our grief with courage and awareness, it can be the key that unlocks our hearts and forces us into a profound new experience of life and love.*

Grief, or loss, has a curious way of breaking down and exposing life in an elemental way. Grief wipes away all pretenses; detects and dismisses the vain, mindless, and inconsequential; and alters our perspectives—so that an overwhelming sense of what *really* matters becomes key to our thoughts and actions.

Grief wipes away all pretenses . . . and alters our perspectives.

Significance becomes a crucial idea we cannot ignore. Our lives have changed forever because we have learned something monumental. Unlearning it is impossible. As Welshons said . . . *"Grief can be our undoing"*—but, it can be so in an amazing way.

When you come to the end of all the light you know, and
    it's time to step into the darkness of the unknown,
faith is knowing that one of two things shall happen: either
    you will be given something solid to stand on or you
    will be taught to fly.

                    —Edward Teller

I challenge you to step into the darkness of the unknown. Experience all God desires and has planned for you. You can be certain the ride will not be boring!

The question becomes, "What is truly significant to you, and what will you do with all you've learned?"

Will you take the risk and experience life in a new way—an unfamiliar way? If you never step out and take risks, you never really live.

> Life is either a daring adventure, or nothing.
> —Helen Keller

THOUGHT TO WRITE ABOUT

Are you willing to take the risk and start remapping your life?

What is your greatest stumbling block to getting started? Turn it into a stepping stone!

Hope Thought:

Your life will never be the same, but even you may be surprised in ways you never thought possible.

What the caterpillar calls the end of the world, the master calls the butterfly.

—RICHARD BACH

18

LAUGHTER—UNBELIEVABLE "MEDICINE"

If we couldn't laugh, we would all go insane.

—JIMMY BUFFETT

The value of laughter is immeasurable—in its proper time, that is. Please understand that I recognize *a time will come* during your grief experience when laughter will again be possible and seem appropriate, but in no way am I dismissing or discounting profound feelings of sadness and loss that accompany your grief. Laughter will not feel comfortable right away.

When painful and catastrophic events occur, even the *possibility* of laughter seems far removed; however, research shows that humor is beneficial in relieving tension, anxiety, and depressive moods.

Richard Williams, in an article from the May 2002 issue of *Parks & Recreation* magazine, discusses the use of therapeutic recreation and humor in treating depression and anxiety:

Depression and anxiety are among the most common charac-teristics of people seeking therapeutic recreation services, and humor can effectively treat both. By its nature, humor seems plainly incompatible with depression . . . Researchers have reported that people with strong senses of humor are less likely to experience depression and more likely to experience higher levels of emotional stability.

. . . Professionals should be attuned to the emotional state of participants. It is contrary to therapeutic goals if participants perceive that their pain is not taken seriously.

Grief requires special handling with regard to humor. And when interacting with someone who is grieving, *sensitivity* to timing, feel-ings, and state of mind is an important concern for loved ones and professionals alike. Grievers need to believe their pain is genuinely recognized, or the effects of laughter can be adverse.

> After a loss, a certain amount of time and distance are necessary before laughter is possible; however, grievers desperately need to find relief from their all-encompassing pain.

Therapeutic recreation can show up in many forms—from orga-nized classes, seminars, or programs, all the way to an individual simply seeking ways to add humor to his life. Reintroducing laughter not only brings optimism to a griever but also is highly constructive. Laughter will help to maintain enough strength to go through the painful and exhausting grieving process.

Laughter Is Essential to Healing—and It also Feels Good

Laughter is a "healing" escape. Since its benefits are so great, think about programming laughter into your life—*intentionally!* Whatever you have to do to make it happen, be certain to include laughter as a regular part of your life.

Laughter not only brings optimism to a griever but also . . . will help to maintain enough strength to go through the painful and exhausting grieving process.

Many grievers allow laughter or humor to cause feelings of guilt and disloyalty. How could I laugh when the person who made me laugh the most was gone? At first, laughter seemed disrespectful. But logic makes more sense than emotion. My husband loved to have a good time, and his joyful attitude was naturally engaging. Deep inside, I knew that he would want me to be happy. *He* would have been telling me to find ways to laugh!

Let go of guilty thoughts. It's okay to laugh. More than okay, it will *boost* your healing. You need moments—and intervals—of relief from your pain.

Well-documented research confirms the powerful therapeutic benefits of laughter. Laughter really is a miracle drug. It's free, has no known negative side effects, is readily available, and it produces an amazing range of positive effects. Laughter . . .

- Improves health
- Stimulates the immune system
- Increases natural killer cells that fight disease
- May reduce the risk of heart disease
- Lowers blood pressure

- Enhances respiration, circulation, and blood flow
- Reduces problems with high blood pressure, strokes, ulcers, and arthritis
- Increases heart rate
- Lowers blood-sugar levels

- Stimulates the brain & improves its function
- Enhances the ability to learn
- Releases endorphins (body's natural painkillers)
- Releases harmful negative emotions such as anger, fear, sadness

- Increases energy
- Stimulates digestion
- Relaxes the body
- Reduces stress hormones/lowers anxiety
- Elevates mood & improves disposition

- Is invigorating & pleasurable
- Can give us a total-body aerobic workout
- Produces effects resembling deep breathing
- Burns calories (ten to fifteen minutes of laughter burns fifty calories)
- One hundred laughs equals 15 minutes on an exercise bike or 10 minutes on a rowing machine

- Is contagious

- Elevates self-esteem

- Connects you to others

- Activates the chemistry of the will to live

- Can change your perspective

- Increases life expectancy

Who would ever guess laughter, of all things, produces so many benefits?

According to Dr. Lee S. Berk, a well-known researcher who has extensively studied the effects of laughter on the immune system, *"If we took what we now know about laughter and bottled it, it would require FDA approval."* This is a powerful statement about what laughter can do!

Dr. William F. Fry, Jr., emeritus professor at Stanford University Medical School, a psychiatrist, and a renowned pioneer (and expert) in humor research, began studying the science of laughter in 1953. Humor therapy has gained greater acceptance over the last twenty-plus years based on studies by numerous researchers.

> *Laughter is inner jogging.*
> *—Norman Cousins*

In addition to the healing benefits of laughter, research by respected experts has shown that the combination of humor along with modern medical treatment increases positive outcomes. Various sources have reported the average adult generally laughs a fraction of the amount the average child laughs (fifteen–seventeen times per day for adults versus 300–400 times per day for children)—so considering laughter's miracle benefits, adults may want to try a little harder to laugh *more!*

Dr. Fry also pointed out that laughter is a "total body experience." He [along with others] has revealed the amazing fact that intense laughter, *even if it's faked*, produces the same effects as real laughter. So what are you waiting for?

> Since your body cannot distinguish between a sincere and a fake laugh, do whatever it takes to laugh—because your body will still receive the benefits.

Make full use of laughter's good medicine. You will not only feel better, but your body will be healthier because of it!

Laughter Fights Disease

Norman Cousins, M.D., became a widely recognized doctor after publishing his research on laughter therapy and hope. He conducted research to find ways to fight his own disease—and he employed this therapy on himself, as well as his patients, in the valiant effort to overcome grave illnesses. In an interview for the Winter 1988 issue of *Whole Earth Review*, Dr. Cousins said:

> *I've come to this conclusion while conducting research at a medical school. I have found verification for a thesis I proposed 10 years ago, namely, that emotions, thoughts, attitudes, and moods have biological effects. The belief there was such a thing as a biology of hope was central in my quest. Now after ten years, we're beginning to see the specific scientific evidence that this thesis is correct. The immune system can be affected by depression on the downside, by hope on the upside.*

I am putting my emphasis these days on the need to persuade people that they have the capacity to beat large problems . . . because in these past forty years, I've learned that next to the atomic bomb the greatest danger is defeatism, despair, and inadequate awareness of what human beings possess. I feel that any problem that can be defined is capable of being resolved. Out of this has come my conviction that no man knows enough to be a pessimist.

Human beings are amazingly powerful. They just have to recognize and *believe* in their abilities to overcome the problems and circumstances they encounter.

Scientific evidence has finally confirmed that emotions, moods, thoughts, and attitudes have biological effects.

There *is* a biology of hope. And it is compelling.

Humor Can Help with Our Struggles

When a well-developed sense of humor characterizes your overall perspective, positive effects will radiate throughout all parts of your life. Science links a good sense of humor to:

- Happiness and well-being
- Success
- Health and physical healing
- Longevity

- Greater creativity

- Better job performance and improved productivity

- Better problem-solving

- Better coping skills

- Greater self-esteem

- More control over your life

- Improved relationships

- A more positive outlook on life

No matter how you look at it, a sense of humor is personally beneficial—all the way around. A positive outlook produces a more healthy overall perspective, and our perceptions affect *everything!* If you want to *be* happy, start thinking happy thoughts . . . and develop a *habit* of laughter and optimistic thinking.

> *A strong positive mental attitude will create more miracles than any wonder drug.*
> —*Patricia Neal*

The good news is that you can develop a good sense of humor—you do not have to be born with it! The Bible even talks about the benefit of a happy heart.

A cheerful disposition is good for your health; gloom and doom leave you bone-tired.

—Proverbs 17:22 (*MSG*)

Laughter has been shown, time and again, to be valuable mentally, physically, emotionally, socially, and spiritually.

Laughter has healing power.

And laughter simply makes us feel good.

If Necessary, Act Your Way into a Feeling

Grief can be draining and seem utterly hopeless, so it is easy to fall prey to our own attitudes, moods, and thoughts. Sometimes we simply need to act our way into a feeling. Make the conscious effort to act, even though you do not feel it, *until the feeling becomes real.*

Have you ever tried to remain angry or unhappy when you are hysterically laughing? Or to remain sad when you force a big smile? These opposing emotions are incompatible. Test it and see for yourself.

You *can* act your way into a feeling. This action does not imply that you are to deny your grief. You still need to work through it. However, you also need *relief* as you heal. Try to remember a time when you laughed with your loved one, or think about something that was funny to them. Perhaps smiling about a funny situation you shared may lead to laughter.

> *Emotions follow actions. To change your emotions, change your actions.*
> *—Edwin Louis Cole*

My husband, John, was a tall, muscular, athletic man (the football-player type) but when something really tickled him, he giggled. His giggle, coupled with his appearance, seemed strangely contradictory but the combination endeared him to others—and his laughter was catching. I still smile when I picture him giggling.

Laughter is an emotional release and a necessary relief. Relief from pain will help to keep hope alive in your heart. And hope is critical. It keeps you going.

Hope is as essential to life as the air we breathe and the water our bodies require. If we allow hope to die, we lose the life force within that pushes us forward even when we think we cannot go on.

Aristotle said, "*Hope is a waking dream.*" So keep dreaming—and do not let anything or anyone stop you.

Believe you have a future. Think about what is good in your life. *Set your mind on something—anything—positive.* Fight fervently to hang on to hope.

There Is Life after Grief

Laughter . . . hope . . . courage . . . perseverance . . . life. There is a future beyond grief—and it is worth keeping on—to reach your tomorrow. Even if you do not yet believe you have a life after grief or that it's worth the effort, consider the words of others who have traveled the path ahead of you. Believe the truths they have discovered.

After attending a grief-support group, a young woman who lost her sister wrote, "*I feel like I went through the eye of the storm into rays of sunshine again . . . I can smile again and it really feels good.*"

> *Be not afraid of life. Believe that life is worth living, and your belief will help create the fact.*
> —William James

After a ten-week group ended, one woman wrote, "*From grief to laughter! Who would have ever thought?*"

After the utter despair that participants experience in the first weeks of a grief-support group, for a person even to be able to write a statement like the one above, after only ten weeks, is remarkable. Of course, she still had a long way to go—but at least she was able to laugh again.

The battle, at times, seems insurmountable, but the result is worth the fight. *Life* is worth the fight.

A friend wrote a beautiful poem for me soon after John died. At the time, my heart was exceptionally tender, and my feelings were fragile. I read her poem after settling into my seat for a return flight to

California after visiting my family in Kentucky. Tears flowed uncontrollably. My loss was fresh and laughter seemed a million miles away.

I hope that someday your heart will heal
And you'll be able to remember and smile
When you recall the treasures of life
That were yours for only a while.

Love can't be measured by days or years
But by the special times you've had.
Just know that someday you'll smile again
Though now you're still so sad.
I see the pain of loss in your eyes
But I also see strength and will.
Try to remember when it hurts so much
That someday your heart will heal.
Did I know you before along the ravels of time
Did we ever just laugh and play
Did we ever tell secrets as only friends can
And didn't we have lots to say.

It's strange how you meet someone in life
And you know their feelings and where they've been.
It seems I have known you a long, long time
I just can't remember where or when.

—Jan Manaway (July 1998)

> *In the depths of winter I finally learned there was in me an invincible summer.*
> *—Albert Camus*

When I first read Jan's poem, I wondered if I would ever laugh again. Would I ever *want* to laugh again?

In time, however, smiles and laughter did return for me—just as they have for others who have experienced the pain of grief. They will return for you, too.

You can make it. You really can. You *can*.

Believe it! Help is waiting—you just have to ask. God is right beside you.

If your heart is broken, you'll find God right there;
if you're kicked in the gut, he'll help you catch your breath.

—Psalm 34:18 (*MSG*)

THOUGHT TO WRITE ABOUT

What are you doing to bring laughter into your life?

Laughter is *so* important—make it a priority! Think about what you can do.

Hope Thought:

Try smiling first thing in the morning—and set the tone for your day!

> *We don't laugh because we're happy—we're happy because we laugh.*
>
> —William James

CHAPTER

OUR TIMING—OR GOD'S?

We must let go of the life we have planned, so as to accept the one that is waiting for us.

—JOSEPH CAMPBELL

Unless you want to be continually frustrated and often times discouraged, set aside *your* timing and concentrate on accepting *God's* timing. Rest assured, the two will almost certainly be different (perhaps drastically so).

Even better, set aside thoughts of time altogether! Now, I realize this task may be impossible. People logically focus on timing because we organize our entire lives around time. However, the less you focus on *time* and the more you focus on *living,* the less frustrated you will be.

> One day with the Lord is like a thousand years,
>   and a thousand years are like one day.
> The Lord isn't slow to do what he promised, as some people
>   think.

—II Peter 3:8–9 (*God's Word*)

Learning to rest in God does not come naturally. In fact, our inborn tendencies are opposite. We aim to be self-sufficient and in control of everything. Sometimes we drive ourselves crazy striving to get ahead—juggling, maneuvering, and stressing over all the balls we have in the air.

The less you focus on time *and the more you focus on* living, *the less frustrated you will be.*

Slow down and take a deep breath. God does not want us to fill our lives (or even a twenty-four-hour slice) with anxiety and turmoil. He wants us to be at peace and to trust Him completely. In fact, the Bible tells us that worry is sinful. Worry indicates a lack of faith, and in the book of Hebrews (11:6), we read that without faith, it is impossible to please God.

The Bible teaches us to trust Him for everything. We are to tell God what we need, give thanks for what He's already done and what He's going to do . . . and then *let go*, expecting (and knowing) He will take care of us. God *wants* to give us His peace.

Our Way Causes Problems

Many times, as believers, we waste significant time and energy by trying to handle things *our* way. We forget that God's thoughts and His ways are not the same as ours. By trying to keep control in our hands, we miss the fullness of life God promises us in Him. We create pain, discomfort, and unnecessary heartache for ourselves by not trusting in God and His provisions for us.

> "My thoughts are completely different from yours," says the Lord.
> "And my ways are far beyond anything you could imagine."
>
> —Isaiah 55:8 (*NLT*)

God can give us power for living and complete peace if we allow Him to work in us. Satan, the great deceiver, will try to trap us into becoming anxious about everything. If he can agitate us and create apprehension, then we will not be in a place of trust where we can hear God's voice. The enemy will then have succeeded in diverting us from God and setting our minds on a turbulent course.

Often, we push ourselves into positions where we are stirred up over the past, reliving and rehashing regrets or "should haves," or worrying about how we are going to handle the future. Spending time thinking about the past or fretting about the future prevents us from living in the present.

> Worry is like a rocking chair. It gives you something to do, but it doesn't get you anywhere.
> —Anonymous

Worry Is Unproductive

We have to keep reminding ourselves that worry is useless and ineffective. Most of what we worry about never happens anyway—but we get ourselves hopelessly caught up and buried with anxiety.

The next time worry overtakes you, try thanking God *specifically* for things you appreciate and for times He has helped you before. Soon your worries fall aside because your focus shifts from yourself (and your problems) to God and your blessings. Thoughts move from a position of need to one of power, abundance, and unlimited provision. Instead of fretting, you're plugging into your Source.

Remain Faithful to God

All God requires is that we believe and trust Him. God's responsibility is to refine us from within—to make us into a new creation. This job is not ours to do, but by trusting in Him, we open the pipeline so that His power can flow into us.

Faith activates the power of God to work within us. Scripture proclaims the outcome:

> . . . when you received the message of God [which you
>   heard] from us,
> you welcomed it not as the word of [mere] man, but as it
>   truly is,
> the Word of God, which is effectually at work in you who
>   believe
> [exercising its superhuman power in those who adhere to
>   and trust in and rely on it].
>
> I Thessalonians 2:13 (AMP)

When we remain faithful to God in our present circumstances (and keep good attitudes, regardless of our situations) we pass God's tests. He constantly stretches us to determine our readiness and to prepare us for what He has planned.

Being faithful means that we realize God has *allowed* our situations, so we trust Him to bring us through them. We ask Him to show us what He wants us to learn. And we seek His guidance as we work our way through.

> Faith *activates the power of God to work within us.*

I cannot change myself, but I can submit to God's will and allow Him to make me into the person He wants me to be. How? Talk to God. Acknowledge *who He is*—and His role in my life. Be receptive and attentive. Ask Him to change my desires, control my thoughts, and guide my actions. Stay connected with Him during the day by uttering short prayers.

Trust and thanks open our hearts to God.

Faith is a journey of learning to follow God one step at a time. *Expect* Him to work in your life—and *thank* Him when He does. The Bible teaches that God dwells in the praises of His people. Calling on His name activates the conduit to His presence and opens our hearts to receive from Him.

The Bible assures us of God's transforming power:

> Don't copy the behavior and customs of this world, but let God transform you into a new person by changing the way you think . . .
>
> —Romans 12:2 (*NLT*)

> For God is working in you, giving you the desire to obey him and the power to do what pleases him.
>
> —Philippians 2:13 (*NLT*)

The Amazing Grace of God

Because of a wrong attitude and failure to obey God, the Israelites had no choice but to wander around the desert for forty years! An entire generation of stubborn, disobedient people had to die before God allowed the new generation to enter the Promised Land. Only two people of the original group—Joshua and Caleb—remained faithful and inherited the land God had promised them.

At first glance, the outcome of this journey may seem harsh. The rest of the story, however, shows the amazing love and Grace of God.

Even though His people were fully rebellious, God watched over them and took care of *all* their needs. He did not desert them and He did not forget about them. You can read the whole account in Nehemiah 9, but this excerpt describes the extent of God's presence and concern: ". . . *Because of your great compassion you did not abandon them . . . For forty years you sustained them in the desert; they lacked nothing, their clothes did not wear out nor did their feet become swollen*" (Nehemiah 9:19, 21, *NIV*).

God can use everything . . . even our greatest tragedy or pain— to bring about something good.

In spite of their defiance, God took care of them. They didn't receive His best (the Promised Land), but He loved them still. Their story exemplifies the unbelievable kind of love He wants to show you.

Be open to how God wants to work for your good. He can use *everything* in our lives—even the greatest tragedy or pain—to bring about something good. Trust Him and allow Him to bless you.

Begin to program your mind with the truth of the following affirmations:

> When the time is right, *nothing* can shut a door that God wants to open. *No* obstacle is too great for God! By a single act, God can change your circumstances *instantly, dramatically, and completely*! God can change anything *at any time*.

Our Expectations Activate God's Power

Practice letting faith and hope hold you captive! *Learn* to expect the best because God will meet you at the level of your expectations.

Thank God ahead of time for His favor. Search the Bible for God's promises and then claim them in prayer. Let God know you're grateful that His answer is on its way. Stay confident. Take steps that show you expect God to act on whatever He has planted in your heart—and talk about these expectations with others. Keep trusting God to act.

According to the Bible, we get to *choose* how much God blesses us. When we have faith we please God—and we are alert and responsive to His working in us.

Expect God to turn things around and make changes in you and for your own good. Count on what the Bible says.

What area(s) of your life do you need to release to God's timing? Can you release them? If not, what is keeping you from doing so?

Talk to God about your issues.

THOUGHT TO WRITE ABOUT

Hope Thought:

God sees the big picture and knows what is best for you. Depend on Him!

Even when it seems like nothing is happening, with God, something is *always* happening!

Because of your faith, it will happen.

—Matthew 9:29 (*NLT*)

CHAPTER

20

....

LEARNING TO EMBRACE SOLITUDE

....

*Life isn't about finding yourself. Life is about creating
yourself.*

—George Bernard Shaw

Take the time and accept the responsibility to look within and
rediscover the person you *really* are. As mates, sometimes we try
to accommodate our spouses' needs and preferences and we forget
about our own. We can become so wrapped up in other people (often
instinctively or subconsciously) that we adapt to their desires and set
ours aside, losing part of who we are in the process. Over time, our
compromising behaviors can become so complete that we essentially
forget our hopes . . . and ourselves.

Search who you are and honestly get to know yourself again.
What are your deepest needs and goals? What do you genuinely enjoy
doing? Explore your strengths and weaknesses. Refine your skills or
develop some new ones. Be fully honest. If you discover places where
you need to grow or change, tackle them. Remember the goal—to

Look within and rediscover the person you really are.

unmask the real you, so you can shape a more satisfying life.

A widow named Kim became a friend after attending a grief workshop. She told me about personal insights she has noticed since the unexpected death of her husband. She suddenly realized that, in many ways, she does not actually know who she is. She said, "*I never took the time to be me—it never occurred to me that that was an option. I have always been someone for somebody.*"

Kim is now on a stimulating voyage of rediscovering herself and her life. She wrote:

"Now I view things differently . . . I see God really cares for me, for who I am, which I never really thought about before. I see him answering the smallest requests . . .

I have the chance to look at my life and respond. There is no one to tell me anything but God, and I rely solely on God. It's a little awesome to think that God cares about me, he really does. I notice him showing me all the time.

I never took the time before, but now I have the time, and I want to see God. And you know what I have discovered? God is a 'show off.' It's kinda amazing how personal God can be . . . Now that life has taken a different path, my God has become more personal and I am finding out who I am. And God is helping me do that."

Kim responded to her painful circumstance in a positive, healthy way. She now has the opportunity to explore new things, possibly even discover unknown talents and interests, and experience life with a fresh approach. Nothing is blocking her path or preventing her from creating a different life of her own design. The excitement in her voice was contagious and inspiring! She has uncovered another springboard of hope for her future.

> One of the greatest moments in anybody's developing experience is when he no longer tries to hide from himself but determines to get acquainted with himself as he really is.
> —Norman Vincent Peale

Learn to Appreciate Solitude

Work on getting comfortable with being alone in your home—without the noise and distraction of the television or music or *busyness*.

I realized I was actually healing when I could be alone in my home again, *in the quiet*, and feel comfortable and serene. When the silence no longer felt awkward or empty, but peaceful, a major change had occurred. What a relief to realize I actually enjoyed being home again! Home *should* feel like a sanctuary, a shelter, a retreat. Solitude *can* be wonderful.

> Solitude is not loneliness; loneliness is the pain of being alone.
> Solitude is the glory of being alive.
> In solitude, you find time to think and take stock of your life.

From: *Living When a Loved One Has Died* by Earl A. Grollman
Copyright © 1977 by Earl A. Grollman
Reprinted by permission of Beacon Press, Boston

I met a kind, middle-aged widow named Tess. She lives in a charming cottage near the beach, but without her husband there too, she describes her home as a prison. Obviously, the comfortable home she formerly loved has not changed—but since she is now alone, it feels like a prison to her.

> *I realized I was healing when I could be alone in my home again,* in the quiet, *and feel comfortable and serene.*

Grief tends to change the way we see things. Tess's home now feels far removed from a refuge. In fact, she does all she can to avoid being there. Solitude means loneliness to her.

Running and trying to hide from grief is usually easier than facing straight on the deeply painful unpleasantness and making difficult changes. People can successfully dodge hurdles for years, but the hurdles do not go away. If you do not face them, they become obstacles that block healing, and peace remains elusive and unattainable. In the words of L.A. Rouchefoliocauld, *"When a man finds no peace within himself, it is useless to seek it elsewhere."*

Use Gratitude and Affirmations to Reprogram Your Mind

Start to affirm and to *expect* that you will again be content in your home. "My home is a safe, peaceful retreat that nourishes me. I love the solitude I find there. Solitude is a *gift* I treasure." Affirm *aloud* that you enjoy being there—because something powerful happens when you actually speak the words. "I love spending time at home."

Express gratitude that you have the opportunity to take some time to explore who you are and develop new interests. Affirm yourself!

Build a *gratitude list*. Pick up a small notebook and start jotting down your blessings—the people (and things) that you appreciate and value most. Review the list—and *commit* each day to add *some-*

thing new. Start expressing your gratitude to God for all the blessings in your life.

By focusing on your blessings instead of your losses, you *can* reprogram your mind. Then, you will begin to see your attitude change. Remember that sometimes you must *act* your way into a feeling.

Your Attitude Can Transform Your Life

The impact of attitude on life may be more important than almost anything else we can think of. Often times, the decisive factor in success, happiness, or overcoming adversity is attitude. How else can we explain why some people successfully rise from negative, devastating circumstances while others become bitter and defeated?

> *Reflect on your present blessings, of which every man has many; not on your past misfortunes, of which all men have some.*
> —Charles Dickens

Nurture an attitude of thankfulness, and see how your outlook changes.

> Be thankful.
> Cultivate an "attitude of gratitude."
> Thankfulness is much more dependent on attitude than
>   circumstance.
> When you feel the lack of what you don't have, thank God
>   for what you do have!
> At any time, there is more going right in the life of a com-
>   mitted Christian than there is going wrong.
> It's just that the "wrong" makes a lot more noise than the
>   "right."
>
> —Jim Stephens
> (FROM *Grace Notes*)

Attitude can transform a person or a situation. Every day we choose how we will respond to what happens to us.

Solitude *can* be a gift.

Look at your situation honestly and, if necessary, begin to change. *You* can make the positive difference that transforms the way you live and respond to your surroundings.

THOUGHT TO WRITE ABOUT

Are you comfortable with solitude?

If so, talk about its blessings. If not, discuss your discomfort—and the steps you can take to conquer it.

Hope Thought:

God speaks in a still small voice. He will not shout to us above the noise and busyness of our lives.

Quiet yourself—and then *listen for His voice!*

"Be silent, and know that I am God!"

—Psalm 46:10 (*NLT*)

CHAPTER

21

. . . .

METAMORPHOSIS—FROM
PAIN TO NEW BEGINNINGS

. . . .

A New Song . . . of Life

Like the rhythmic persistence
of raindrops falling on a tin roof,
Life *fights* to be heard
above the aftermath of death.

Life whispers, calls, *urges* . . .
Draw closer. Look deeper.
Risk higher. Cherish more.
Sing *a new song*.

—JUDY BRIZENDINE

Other experiences in life may ignite signs of metamorphic change, but tragic loss has been my introduction to this evolving process. Initially, I would never have expected even the remote *possibility* of such an outcome. I had no idea that growth, beauty, and wisdom could be byproducts of such intense pain.

Do not be troubled if you cannot see a positive result emerging from your painful experience so far—believe me, I didn't reach this conclusion quickly. In fact, the process has been very slow (probably seven or eight years long—and I am still learning, more than twelve years after my loss). Honestly, I think the progression will continue for the rest of my life. The effort, however, brings unforeseen meaning to life and a worthwhile purpose for continuing the difficult journey.

A Life of Significance

God is a master of new beginnings.

The closer we get to God, the more we want to distance ourselves from trivial, meaningless activities and instead spend our time in ways that make eternal differences. After facing tragic loss, we are more inclined to focus on people, activities, and goals that matter. Above all, we want our lives to be significant.

We want to make a difference.

That is one of God's greatest—and most common—gifts:
    the gift of hope to keep us in the game,
to return us to our places not as the same people we were
    before,
but awake, alive to God's transforming presence in our
    midst.

—James Edwards
(from *The Divine Intruder*)

A word picture and an image can illustrate a griever's evolving path as he or she moves through grief toward healing (remapping). Visualize a slightly flattened diamond shape with rounded corners, but one that does not connect end-to-end. Instead, the line completing the outline of the diamond extends just beyond (and slightly outside) the original starting point near its base, an important distinction you will see in a moment. This line runs parallel to the original one for a short distance—and points upward with an arrow at its end. 'Ripples' fill the diamond's interior. This visual summarizes the remapping process. It is a *symbol of hope*. Plant the picture in your mind. Recall its meaning expressed below. And remember your destination.

Remapping—a Symbol of Hope

At first, because of intense, unrelenting pain, one's focus is *completely* self-centered and stuck on square one. After a while, even though you have started moving around the course, you *feel* as though you're going backward. As you start to heal, *slowly* your focus becomes less self-absorbed. Gradually, as you travel farther along, you realize you *are* moving forward. In time, your attention shifts from the past (and loss) to the future. You become more sensitive to people around you [the ripple effect].

Grief's uneven path—marked by ins and outs, ups and downs— does not fit a perfectly predictable pattern. So instead of a circle, a diamond-like shape represents a more accurate picture of the remapping process.

Eventually, we all need to move full circle—and finally emerge on the other side of grief. However, we don't end up in the places where we started. Instead, we end up *beyond* our starting points—and on slightly different paths (the continuing parallel line, just outside the position where the diamond began). An upward-pointing arrow at the end of the line signifies a new beginning.

After confronting the pain of loss, our perspectives change forever, and our capacities to be human deepen. We now see life through different lenses.

There must *be some purpose in the pain.*

Concern and empathy develop out of our experiences of loss, and the prospect of helping others because of what we have learned and endured becomes a consideration, possibly even a passion.

Ironically, helping others is personally healing. By reaching out to help other people, we are also doing something healthy for ourselves.

When I look for ways to encourage someone else, I temporarily forget about my concerns. When my actions make someone's day better or ease her worry, my attitude *sings*. We both win.

Looking for the blessings that come from pain requires effort, attention, and time. We will not even want to entertain this thought when our pain is fresh and deep. However, having endured the anguish, we long for something positive to come out of it.

There *must* be some purpose in the pain. The purpose is twofold—insight for living life more fully and a deeper relationship with God.

God Is Our Hope

Ultimately, our eternal hope lies in God. The following passage from *The Message* bible translation graphically sums up why we, as believers, have a sound reason to hope:

> When God wanted to guarantee his promises, he gave his
>   word, a rock-solid guarantee—
> God can't break his word.
> And because his word cannot change, the promise is like-
>   wise unchangeable.
> We who have run for our very lives to God
>   have every reason to grab the promised hope with both
>   hands and never let go.
> It's an unbreakable spiritual lifeline, reaching past all
>   appearances
> right to the very presence of God where Jesus, running on
>   ahead of us,
> has taken up his permanent post as high priest for us . . .
>
> —Hebrews 6:18–20 (*MSG*)

God's plan for our lives is a great adventure! Dietrich Bonhoeffer challenges us by his words, *"We must be ready to allow ourselves to be interrupted by God."*

What will you decide to do with what God has allowed you to face? How will you change the way you live?

Has your attitude changed?

Will your relationships now be different?

Will you embrace God's unique plan for you? Will you let God interrupt *your* plans with His?

God's dreams for you are beyond your imagination, and His plans are perfect, complete, and amazing. Phil Munsey, in his groundbreaking book, *Legacy Now,* helps us understand why *everything* about us matters—and that our spiritual destiny is in our DNA! A vital link (through our DNA and our blood) joins each of our lives to God's purpose and plans, and holds the power to transform us completely. Munsey shares these words of challenge, hope, passion, and encouragement:

> *"The biggest thing you could ever imagine happening in your life will fall short of what God wants to do and **will** do if you can see beyond the temporary to envision the eternal.*
>
> *Live your life beyond belief. Believe in yourself as God believes in you. Believe that you can see your dreams come true. Dreams are not just luxuries for the elite while the rest of us drudge through life with pressures and problems too real to escape . . ."*

When you relinquish control to God and see where the path leads, you will be surprised, and you will not be disappointed!

From a practical, human viewpoint, resigning from a leadership position in a respected design firm and pursuing a dream in an untested arena seemed foolish (and probably still does) to many who know me. This book is the result of that decision. The financial impact has been great; however, my husband and I have made adjustments, and God continues to cause our circumstances to work out. Are we in the black every month? No. However, God has taken a situation that logically should *never* have worked (or even come close!) and sustained us. We stepped out in faith. And the adventure continues to unfold. We *expect* God to fulfill dreams that we cannot possibly achieve on our own. But we're marching in that direction and trusting Him to equip and direct us.

What are you waiting for? In the words of Tom Rea, "*Life is no dress rehearsal.*"

What purpose(s) have you found because of your pain?

THOUGHT TO WRITE ABOUT

How will you live your life differently now?

Hope Thought:

Always remember—our God is a God of miracles!

We are all pencils in the hand of God.

—MOTHER TERESA

PART THREE

INTERACTIVE EXERCISES

Remapping Tools

INTERACTIVE EXERCISES:
THE ROAD TO HEALING

*A clay pot sitting in the sun will always be a clay pot.
It has to go through the white heat of the furnace to
become porcelain.*

—MILDRED W. STRUVEN

Unfortunately, many people do not have the opportunity to attend a grief-support group, so they are unable to take advantage of the healing power that comes from sharing their grief openly with others in the same boat.

A powerful alternative for facing and working through issues is journaling. This part of the book provides another path to healing by suggesting more key topics surrounding grief to think about and discuss through writing. Many thoughts, feelings, issues, experiences, and insights arise out of the grief journey.

> *Work through your thoughts the same way you would talk to a trusted friend. Get the feelings out of your head (and heart) onto paper.*

Find a notebook or journal book and just start writing. Write your thoughts about the questions and hope statements at the end of each chapter, as well as the questions found here. Jot down anything that comes to mind. Also, write about whatever you are thinking or feeling throughout your time of recovery and renewal.

Work through your thoughts in the same way you would talk to a trusted friend. Get the feelings out of your head (and heart) onto paper—and experience the relief that comes from confronting and releasing these issues and emotions. Try it!

While this thought may sound simplistic, Joseph Compton's statement, *"An avalanche begins with a snowflake,"* is true—not only in and of itself, but also in relation to healing.

> Small steps seem ineffective and unnoticeable at first; however, they eventually produce an unmistakable effect.

Another benefit of journaling is that your strength and optimism will grow as you go back and read the words you wrote earlier in your journey. You will be able to trace your thread of progress and will have indisputable evidence that you are healing. This proof will be an important reminder, especially on inescapable "down" days. Your faith will grow stronger as you recognize signs of God moving in your life.

I recently read some journal entries from several years ago, and they are a treasured record of special times I spent with God—as well as a demonstration of my faith changing and developing, bit by bit. My only regret is that I have not consistently journaled over the years.

Following is an entry I wrote almost two years after John died:

Personal Journal Entry—January 8, 2000

Today, I was feeling very alone and lonely. I felt as though God was not paying attention to me. I prayed that He would get involved—and bring others into my life for companionship and love. I asked why God allowed these circumstances [widowhood and the resulting challenges], and what He wants to teach me through all of this. Maybe it's just to look to Him—the only one with the power and ability to meet every need I have.

*When I sat down to read my Bible, I suddenly realized God **was** paying attention and He had not forgotten about me. I read the words, "Regardless of your circumstances, God has not forgotten you. Obey Him and trust in his plan." Wow!*

Thank you, God, for leading me to such faith-building words—words I needed to hear and keep in mind so I don't give up and become discouraged. The Bible also says that even people of great faith may have doubts—but [as believers] we are to focus on Your commitment to fulfill Your promises, and then continue to obey.

I must keep my eyes on God—not on my problems or my needs. Nothing is impossible to God. I just ask that You show me Your love through some other person today. Thank you for revealing Your concern and presence to me through Your Word in such a powerful way—when I so needed to hear from You.

Even today (more than ten years since this entry was written), when I go back and read my journal, I remember God's faithfulness and His answers to prayer. I can see a record of His presence in my life. And when I get discouraged, as we all do, I can read the words I wrote and *recall* concrete reasons I have to be confident today.

Just when I thought He was ignoring me, He showed me otherwise.

When I needed help the most, God *never* let me down. He arranged the details of the motorhome sale—and effortlessly, miraculously, *everything* fell into place. My car is another example of God's help—and when I needed to sell it, I did not have to advertise or look for a buyer. My mechanic referred the perfect family to purchase my car, and the transaction was seamless. When I stopped striving to find a significant relationship, the man I would finally marry just *showed up*. God is faithful.

He hears the cries of His children:

> *When they call on me, I will answer;*
> *I will be with them in trouble.*

—Psalm 91:15 (*NLT*)

QUESTIONS FOR JOURNALING

These questions relate to various stages of the grief experience. You will be able to face some of the questions in the early days of your journey, but some will only be approachable as you travel farther down the path.

Don't be discouraged. Tackle the questions as you are strong enough to face them—in your own time.

This journey is not a race. There is no time limit.

You set the pace. You determine the direction.

- What am I afraid of?
- What are the greatest adjustments and challenges I have faced so far in my grief?
- Who (or what) surprised or disappointed me the most?
- What is my biggest obstacle to healing? What can I do to get past it?
- How will I know that I am getting better?
- How have my priorities changed because of my loss?

- Self-revelations: What new strengths have I discovered in myself as I have faced my loss?

- What new realities has death forced me to see?

- My "to do" list: practical necessities I need to address because of my loved one's death . . .

- I cannot help but laugh every time I think about . . .

- Things I look forward to now . . .

- How did your death change me? Have I discovered new meaning in life on account of your death?

- Describe a lifetime of precious memories I want to hold onto . . .

- My new life mission is . . .

- I have a dream to . . .

PART
FOUR

HOPE

You Still Have a Future

HOPE FOR YOU

There are only two ways to live your life.
One is as though nothing is a miracle.
The other is as though everything is a miracle.

—ALBERT EINSTEIN

To move forward, sometimes we need a few words to make us smile, a bit of "positive reinforcement" to nudge us along, and someone who understands.

When you need a boost, turn to these pages and start reading! Here you will find encouragement as you read thoughts and heartfelt suggestions written by fellow travelers at various stages in their grief journeys.

> You are not alone. You *can* pull through. Others have been where you are now, and they have found hope.
> This hope is also for you.

Finally, a short collection of positive writings, lessons learned, and powerful verses from the Bible are included to reassure you, build your faith—and stimulate your thinking to new possibilities.

Simply read, savor, and *dream*. Let the optimistic words saturate your mind and provoke your thinking with new seeds of promise and hope.

ENCOURAGEMENT AND SUGGESTIONS FROM GRIEF TRAVELERS

You Are not Alone—Others Have Made It

"Know that you are not alone—and many have fought the battle you're in and have come through to continue with life. Yes, you will have scars, but they will just make you a stronger and better person."

Don't Be Afraid to Talk about Your Loved One

"My five-year-old son and I talk about my husband/his daddy every day. It makes us feel better to share our happy memories and sad and mad feelings about our loss. It feels normal and natural to include his [daddy's] memory throughout our daily activities."

Journaling Helps

"I have a journal where I write letters to my husband whenever the need arises. Putting my feelings down on paper is cathartic."

Don't Try to Hurry Your Grieving

"Don't be in a hurry to try to get your life back to 'normal.' Just go with your feelings as you navigate your way to a 'new normal.' It took me over

six months before I started to pack away only half of the things from my husband's closet."

Pamper Yourself and Help Others

"Engage in activities that make you feel good: exercise, meeting with friends, spa treatments, weekends away, hobbies, etc. Volunteering and helping others in grief takes your mind off of your own pain for a while."

Grieving Is not *a 'Lone Ranger'* Process

"For those of you joining this group [grief-support group], you will find encouragement and insight by being with people who share this same painful chapter in life. I lost my faith in God when I lost my husband, but being part of this group has helped to repair my cold heart and restore my faith.

"Sharing my memories and feelings with people who are grieving is especially helpful and comforting. I've learned that what I'm going through is normal, and I have learned good tools to cope when the sad times hit. This group was a Godsend straight to me. So please hang in there and give it time, and realize that the answer to our pain in our own lives lies within us, as we feel free to give and receive help in an open way."

Grief Takes Time, but a Meaningful New Life Is Possible

"It has been two and one-half years now since my husband passed away. I am left with raising my two sons, ages ten and seven, alone. I put much of my grieving aside, to tend to the everyday living and school activities. I was there for them, putting on the brave face and comforting them, telling them it would be all right.

"Now, after two and one-half years, I realized I need to address my loss head-on. I don't cry as much anymore, and my memories of our life together are very precious. I have taken baby steps forward, just a little at a time, to try and accomplish things on my own.

"I have hope that there is a life for me without him. At first, I was content to stay living in the memories, but now I realize he would not want me to mourn for the rest of my life. He would not want me and our sons to be unhappy because he was not there. He loved us too much for that. So I am going forward.

"I, like many of you, was stuck for a long while. But now I can see that there is my life to be lived . . . A life that is different, finding meaning in different things from what we knew before.

"I have come to know that it is best to reach out to people for help and to help others. I relish my family relationships and friendships. I do not take any relationships for granted. Especially my sons.

"Thank you, dear God, for loving me and showing me there is hope, love, and strength in You."

Victor or Victim? It's a Choice Every Day

"I wanted to share with you what I learned through this grief-support group. When I first came, it was so hard to get out of my car and walk into this group.

"I was so devastated by the loss of my husband and the previous two years of pain and turmoil cancer brought into our lives. I am a stay-at-home mom with two children, five and six years old. I felt scared and was clutching a small thread to keep me going. I hung onto my faith in God and my belief that He loved me and has a bigger plan for my life that I can't see now.

"This group gave me a safe place to come and share with people who really understood. I have come so far in ten weeks. This group showed me

that it's a 'choice every day to choose being a victor rather than being a victim.' The more you talk about it, listen to others, and learn, and above all pray and give it to God, the more you're on the way to healing."

There Is Hope—with God, I Can Make It

"There is light at the end of the tunnel. This ten-week group has not ended my grief, but the love and support I received have helped me to face the new chapter in my life . . . I lost my beloved husband seven months ago and have dealt with many challenges that he handled. I never thought I'd get through these hurdles, but God has carried me through. I pray the Lord will wrap His loving arms around you and grant you the peace you're seeking."

Don't Look too Far Ahead and Ask God for Help

"I know your pain! I would like to tell you what has helped me the most thus far. Get through the moment only—try not to look too far ahead. Cry those tears of sorrow. And cry out to God for help and watch how He shows Himself."

Trust Others Who Have Traveled Before You

"I am so tired of the pain and reality of your death. I see your clothes and my heart stops. Everything I see, feel, touch, and smell has a connection to you.

"I don't want to let go of the best thing that ever happened to me, but I am being pulled by the realities of living. I am being encouraged by those who have gone before me.

"I wonder when I will say, 'Enough pain—I choose to live,' as others have in the group."

Similarities and Differences in Grieving

"I learned that my personality 'type' helped me deal with my grief in a way that differs from the others in the group. Each one of us, as grievers, will have our very own personal experiences with grief.

"What we have in common as a group is: We all want to honor our loved ones; we all want to be understood; we all want to find comfort in God, family, and friends . . .

"This will happen, just trust . . . trust God."

This young man explained to me that his personality type enabled him to deal with dramatic changes easier than other personalities; however, his outward appearance sometimes caused others to misinterpret his grieving. Because he *seemed* okay on the outside, they misjudged his grief and mistakenly thought he had easily accepted his loss.

Everyone grieves differently, but we all share similar needs. Misunderstandings may arise when some draw incorrect conclusions about the grief of others.

Grief Is Universal . . . and Personal

"I had to face loneliness, emptiness, a broken heart, unfinished plans and dreams, and learning to live my life as a single person (I hate the word widow).

"I have learned that no two people grieve in the same way. I have learned what not to say to people who are hurting, and to let friends know that it is okay to talk about death and the person who has passed on. I have learned that talking and crying are forms of healing. And, I have learned that life is too short to spend time thinking negative thoughts and feeling sorry for myself.

"God gives us each day and we must make the most of that day. You may think that you have nothing to give, but everyone has something to give. It may be just a smile, hand touch, or it could be a bigger picture. I have learned that once I started giving to others, my heart started healing."

You Are not Alone

"You are not alone . . . others have gone this way before you . . . God IS with you . . . even if you don't always feel Him."

Don't Be Afraid to Talk and Cry

"Talk openly and honestly about your feelings and the one you've lost . . . and it's okay to cry while you do . . . tears are a healing agent."

Don't Be too Hard on Yourself

"You will find times of happiness and contentment . . . but don't be discouraged if and when you feel like you've taken a giant step backward . . . it is natural . . . look for the little ways that you find you are getting better . . . and give yourself a pat on the back."

Use Affirmations (Words of Encouragement) Daily

"Find some words of encouragement that really speak to you . . . and repeat them throughout the day . . . especially when you start to feel down."

Be Gentle with Yourself

"Don't be too hard on yourself . . . this is a very self-centered time in your life . . . treat yourself kindly . . . and let others do the same for you."

You Will Get Better

"God bless you as you travel this most difficult road . . . you WILL get better!"

Finding Peace

"When you lose someone you have loved, it is hard to imagine how you can go on.

"This experience has changed your life. You will grow to have a greater appreciation for family, friends, and special moments. It will always hurt, but you will come to a point where you will find peace."

People just like you wrote these words—people who lost those they loved deeply. All types of people—men and women, single and married, from twenty-something to eighty-something—discovered wisdom and found hope as they journeyed through the trenches of grief. They want to infuse you with their hope.

Believe that you can untangle the chaos of grief and create a new, rewarding life.

These travelers willingly shared their insights about grief because they care about others in pain. They have spoken from experience. They understand. They have already been where you are now.

Read, understand, and *believe* that what is true for them is also true for you. You *can* untangle the chaos of grief and create a new, rewarding life.

> *Faith is to believe what you do not yet see; the reward for this faith is to see what you believe.*
> —St. Augustine

SIGNS OF A NEW BEGINNING

The sun's relentless rays
fractured the heavy clouds
and oppressive gloom,
Peeking through . . .
Brilliantly lighting the sky
as though their very existence
depended on proclaiming
the *hope* of a new beginning.

Hope, always there,
waiting to be summoned . . .
Even when we can't see it.

—JUDY BRIZENDINE

THINGS I'VE LEARNED ABOUT GRIEF

- Grief does not last forever—even though sometimes it seems so
- The end of something signals the beginning of another
- Grief is not a four-letter word
- Grief changes people—the "how" is up to you
- We *need* each other—grief is too hard to do alone
- You have to *feel* the pain to heal from the pain
- Talk it out, write it out, cry it out, and get it out
- Time does *not* heal all wounds
- Your grief is unique, but it's also universal
- No one understands as does someone else going through it
- Grief involves work—don't let anyone try to fool you
- Grief is unlike anything you can imagine
- Grief changes some of your relationships
- Grief will not just go away

- Be intentional . . . do something . . . take an *active* role in your grief

- What you do makes a difference

- Ask yourself, "Do I really want to get well?"

- Help will come from unexpected places

- Grief's eventual imprint on your life may surprise you

- There is life B.G. (before grief) and A.G. (after grief)— you can't go back . . . and you can't *unlearn* what you now know

- Change is inevitable—so try to embrace it

- Remember to laugh

- Trust God

- You're stronger than you think

- Life *can* be meaningful again

- The pain won't last forever

- You *will* make it through

- This, too, shall pass . . .

- Spend some time every day with God, and He'll help you find a new reason for living

- You don't need enough courage for the rest of your life—you only need enough for *today*

- Each day is a new day . . . and a new chance to begin again

- Life is worth fighting for—*your* life is worth fighting for

- God still does miracles

THE RIPPLE EFFECT

Each choice we make
causes a ripple effect in our lives.
When things happen to us,
it is the reaction we choose
that can create the difference between
the sorrows of our past
and the joy in our future.

—© 2003 CHELLE THOMPSON,
www.InspirationLine.com

YOUR DESTINY

Watch your thoughts,
They become your words.

Watch your words,
They become your actions.

Watch your actions,
They become your habits

Watch your habits,
They become your character.

Watch your character,
It becomes your destiny.

—UNKNOWN AUTHOR

HOPE FROM GOD'S WORD

Acceptance

But you'll welcome us with open arms when we run for
cover to you.

—Psalm 5:11 (*MSG*)

Fulfillment

God made my life complete when I placed all the pieces
before him.

—Psalm 18:20 (*MSG*)

Safety and Provision

My help and glory are in God—granite-strength and
safe-harbor-God—
So trust him absolutely, people; lay your lives on the line
for him.
God is a safe place to be.

—Psalm 62:7–8 (*MSG*)

Trust

I hold on to you for dear life, and you hold me steady as a post.

—Psalm 63:8 (*MSG*)

Open up before God, keep nothing back;
he'll do whatever needs to be done . . .

—Psalm 37:5 (*MSG*)

Protection

He ordered his angels to guard you wherever you go.
If you stumble, they'll catch you; their job is to keep you
    from falling.

—Psalm 91:11–12 (*MSG*)

God guards you from every evil, he guards your very life.
He guards you when you leave and when you return,
he guards you now, he guards you always.

—Psalm 121:7–8 (*MSG*)

God's Presence

If God hadn't been there for me, I never would have made it.
The minute I said, "I'm slipping, I'm falling," your love,
    God, took hold and held me fast.
When I was upset and beside myself, you calmed me down
    and cheered me up.

—Psalm 94:17–19 (*MSG*)

Hope

Unrelenting disappointment leaves you heartsick,
but a sudden good break can turn life around.

—Proverbs 13:12 (*MSG*)

Humanly speaking, it is impossible. But with God everything is possible.

—Matthew 19:26 (*NLT*)

Do not be afraid! Don't be discouraged . . . for the battle is not yours, but God's.

—II Chronicles 20:15 (*NLT*)

God's Power

"You're blessed when you're at the end of your rope.
With less of you there is more of God and his rule."

—Matthew 5:3 (*MSG*)

Assurance

No one's ever seen or heard anything like this,
Never so much as imagined anything quite like it—
What God has arranged for those who love him.

—I Corinthians 2:9 (*MSG*)

Eternity

God's Law is more real and lasting than the stars in the sky
    and the ground at your feet.
Long after stars burn out and earth wears out, God's Law
    will be alive and working.

—Matthew 5:18 (MSG)

Grace

"Are you tired? Worn out? Burned out on religion?
Come to me.
Get away with me and you'll recover your life.
I'll show you how to take a real rest.
Walk with me and work with me—watch how I do it.
Learn the unforced rhythms of grace.
I won't lay anything heavy or ill-fitting on you.
Keep company with me and you'll learn to live freely and
    lightly."

—Matthew 11:28–30 (MSG)

Power

God can do anything, you know—far more than you could
    ever imagine or guess or request in your wildest dreams!
He does it not by pushing us around but by working within
    us, his Spirit deeply and gently within us.

—Ephesians 3:20 (MSG)

Faith

The fundamental fact of existence is that this trust in God,
    this faith,
is the firm foundation under everything that makes life
    worth living.
It's our handle on what we can't see.

—Hebrews 11:1 (*MSG*)

Peace

Never worry about anything.
But in every situation let God know what you need
    in prayers and requests while giving thanks.
Then God's peace, which goes beyond anything we can
    imagine,
will guard your thoughts and emotions through Christ
    Jesus.

—Philippians 4:6–7 (*God's Word*)

Savior and God

. . . No god was formed before me, and there will be none
    after me.
I alone am the Lord, and there is no savior except me.

—Isaiah 43:10b–11 (*God's Word*)

My purpose in writing is simply this: that you who believe
in God's Son
will know beyond the shadow of a doubt that you have
eternal life,
the reality and not the illusion.
And how bold and free we then become in his presence,
freely asking according to his will, sure that he's listening.
And if we're confident that he's listening, we know that
what we've asked for is as good as ours.

—I John 5:13–15 (*MSG*)

Hope and Redemption

"Don't be afraid, I've redeemed you. I've called you by
name.
You're mine.
When you're in over your head, I'll be there with you.
When you're in rough waters, you will not go down.
When you're between a rock and a hard place, it won't be a
dead end—
Because I am God, your personal God, The Holy of Israel,
your Savior.
I paid a huge price for you:
. . . *That's* how much you mean to me! *That's* how much I
love you!
I'd sell the whole world to get you back, trade the creation
just for you."

—Isaiah 43:1–4 (*MSG*)

Our hope . . . our help . . . our security . . . our lives . . . more than we can imagine, and all we'll ever need. God.

And what's so astounding is that we mean *everything* to Him. You and I mean *everything* to the God of the Universe.

PSALM 23

God, my shepherd!
I don't need a thing.
You have bedded me down in lush meadows,
you find me quiet pools to drink from.
True to your word,
you let me catch my breath
and send me in the right direction.

Even when the way goes through
Death Valley,
I'm not afraid
when you walk at my side.
Your trusty shepherd's crook
makes me feel secure.

You serve me a six-course dinner
right in front of my enemies.
You revive my drooping head;
my cup brims with blessing.

Your beauty and love chase after me
every day of my life.
I'm back home in the house of God
for the rest of my life.

—PSALM 23:1–6 (*MSG*)

EPILOGUE

*The capacity for hope is the most significant fact
of life. It provides human beings with a sense of
destination and the energy to get started.*

—NORMAN COUSINS

Bernie Siegel, M.D., a retired surgeon, author, and dedicated
human being, has passionately spread his message about *"how
our mind influences our body and how to use this knowledge to our
advantage."* While Dr. Siegel is widely known for treating and counseling exceptional patients, notably those with cancer, he has uncovered powerful concepts that deliver hope and life-embracing change
to anyone. Enthusiastic, courageous attitudes toward life typify
exceptional patients.

Hidden within disease, death, and tragedy are "gifts" of transfor-
mation. Taken from his book, *Peace, Love & Healing,* Bernie's words
reflect my sentiments about grief: *"There will always be loss and grief. I
know, however, that out of pain new love and true healing can occur . . .
The path is difficult but it will lead to moments of great beauty."*

More than twelve years have passed since John suddenly died and much has happened, including the death of my dearly loved father. I was still grieving for my husband when my dad died two-and-a-half years later. Even though Dad courageously fought multiple life-threatening illnesses for several years, the final development that took his life came quickly and without warning.

Death *demands* our attention—we cannot avoid or postpone it. However, in the pain, God has been faithful to me.

Once I surrendered my future to God and accepted His will (even if it turned out to be different from mine), things began to change. I met a wonderful Christian man, a widower, and discovered we share the same beliefs, goals, and interests. A year later, Jon and I were married, and in September 2010, we celebrated our eighth anniversary! Gratefully, I married a man I love to laugh with—who also understands my deepest hurt. I am happy that God's plan for me included marriage.

God's timing and His plans are perfect. For some time, Jon and I wanted to serve in a ministry together but could not find the right opportunity. He traveled frequently, but even when in town, his ever-changing schedule kept us from committing. When his company forced a strike ["lockout"], he was temporarily unemployed. Almost immediately after the lockout, a leader in our church called Jon to ask if we would facilitate a grief-support workshop. Without hesitation he said, "Yes!" So we started leading a support group.

We facilitated groups at Saddleback Church for more than two years. God graciously allowed us to help other grieving people—but He blessed us more than we could have imagined.

We were honored to share God's love with others during their times of intense pain, and we're thankful to have contributed to their healing. God performed miracles in our groups, transforming people's ideas, pain, relationships, and lives right before our eyes. This book is an outgrowth of the work God began with the support groups.

Jon and I passionately believe grief education is sorely needed—both within the Christian and secular communities, and among clergy, professionals, and people in general. The gravity and repercussions of deep grief are impossible for the uninitiated to grasp.

> Countless problems people face—often without knowing it—center on grief. Healing and restoration from grief are necessary for emotional, relational, spiritual, and physical health.

Grief affects every area of one's life. And sooner or later everyone will experience profound loss. Since death is inescapable, each of us will inevitably lose someone we love dearly. As the largest segments of our population age, the sheer number of individuals who encounter grief will increase dramatically. Each of us will also face devastating losses of many types that are not associated with death—but are still grief.

Given that the effects of loss are far-reaching, and our society is ill-equipped to deal with grief—an ever-growing need exists for people to learn about the subject.

We need to understand grief, not only for our own benefits, but to support friends and family when grief invades. Waiting to be ambushed by death or loss is setting us up for anguish that is partially avoidable. If we can prevent *at least some* of our distress by learning about grief, the effort is worthwhile.

My prayer is that God will use this book to spread knowledge, hope, understanding, and encouragement to hurting people who must face the challenge of working through their losses.

My prayer is also that God will use the book throughout the world to activate discussion and focus attention on grief—and to help change the way people view one of the toughest experiences each of us will face. Our goal is to help more and more people find pathways to healing, prompting them, in turn, to help others—thus completing the circle of God's love.

May God's special blessings be yours! Thank you for allowing me to enter into your personal grief experience.

—Judy Brizendine

When walking through the "valley of shadows,"
remember, a shadow is cast by a Light.

—H. K. Barclay

ENDNOTES

Introduction

1. Joan Didion, *The Year of Magical Thinking* (New York, NY: Alfred A. Knopf, a division of Random House, Inc., 2005), 3.

Chapter 1

What Does Grief Look Like—and How Does It Progress?

1. Toby Talbot, *A Book About My Mother*. Originally published (New York: Farrar Straus & Giroux, 1980), 16.
2. Jeremiah 29:11 (*MSG*)

Chapter 2

How Do I Respond to Grief?

1. Dr. Henry Cloud and Dr. John Townsend, *How People Grow* (Grand Rapids, MI: Zondervan, 2001), 227–228.
2. Ibid., 228.
3. Earl A. Grollman, *Living When a Loved One Has Died* (Boston, MA: Beacon Press, 1995), 15–17.
4. Henri J. M. Nouwen, *Out of Solitude* (Notre Dame, IN: Ave Maria Press, 1974), 34.
5. Stephen Arterburn, M.Ed., *Healing Is a Choice* (Nashville, TN: Thomas Nelson, Inc., 2005), 33–34.
6. John E. Welshons, *Awakening from Grief* (Novato, CA: New World Library). Originally published (Makawao, Maui, HI: Inner Ocean Publishing, Inc., © 2003 by John E. Welshons), 10.
7. Jeremiah 31:3, 13 (*MSG*)

Chapter 3

How Do Others Respond to Me?

1. Martha Whitmore Hickman, *Healing After Loss* (New York: Avon Books, Inc., 1994), page June 15. Copyright © Martha Whitmore Hickman. HarperCollins Publishers.

Chapter 4

The Isolation of Grief—a Solitary Journey

1. John W. James and Frank Cherry, *The Grief Recovery Handbook,* (New York, NY: Harper & Row, Publishers, 1988), 56. Copyright © John W. James and Frank Cherry. HarperCollins Publishers.
2. Stanley P. Cornils, *The Mourning After—How To Manage Grief Wisely* (Saratoga, CA: R & E Publishers, 1992), 2.
3. C.S. Lewis, *A Grief Observed,* Copyright © C.S. Lewis Pte. Ltd. 1961. Previously published (New York, NY: HarperSanFrancisco, a division of Harper Collins Publishers, 1961), 24.
4. Janis M. Brizendine, "*What Is to Be?*"
5. Pat Schwiebert and Chuck DeKlyen, *Tear Soup* (Portland, OR: Grief Watch, 2003), 17.
6. Max Lucado, *When God Whispers Your Name* (Nashville, TN: W Publishing Group, a division of Thomas Nelson, Inc., 1994, 1999), 13.
7. Romans 8:38–39 (*NLT*)
8. Dinah Maria Mulock Craik, *A Life for a Life* (New York: Harper & Brothers, Publishers, Franklin Square, 1903), 169.

Chapter 5

Insensitivity—or Lack of Understanding?

1. Dr. Sidney B. Simon and Suzanne Simon, *Forgiveness: How to Make Peace with Your Past and Get On with Your Life* (New York: Grand Central Publishing, 1991), 19.
2. Ephesians 1:19 (*NLT*)

Chapter 6

Why Am I Afraid?—and How Do I Conquer My Fear?

1. Alla Bozarth-Campbell, Ph.D., *Life Is Goodbye/Life Is Hello: Grieving Well Through All Kinds of Loss* (Center City, MN: Hazelden Educational Materials, 1994), 37.

Chapter 7

Pivotal Question: Do I Really Want to Get Well?

1. Rick Pitino with Bill Reynolds, *Success Is A Choice* (New York, NY: Broadway Books, 1997), 217–236.
2. Rick Pitino with Pat Forde, *Rebound Rules* (New York, NY: Collins, an imprint of HarperCollins Publishers, 2008), 18–20, 27, 30.
3. http://www.rickpitino.com/rpitino/main.aspx

Chapter 8

Grief Is Active: The Pain (and Reward) of Confrontation

1. Viktor E. Frankl, *Man's Search for Meaning* (New York, NY: Pocket Books, a division of Simon & Schuster, Inc., 1984), 116. (All rights reserved. Copyright © 1959, 1962, 1984, 1992, by Viktor E. Frankl. Beacon Press, 25 Beacon Street, Boston, MA 02108).
2. Psalm 121:3 (*NIV*)
3. Psalm 121:5–6 (*NIV*)
4. Jeremiah 6:14 (*TLB*)

Chapter 9

Here I Am, but Where Do I Turn for Help and What Do I Do?

1. Isaiah 46:3–4 (*Good News Bible: TEV*)
2. Ashton Applewhite, William R. Evans III, and Andrew Frothingham, *And I Quote* (New York, NY: St. Martin's Press, 1992), 133.
3. Max Lucado, *The Great House of God* (Nashville, TN: Thomas Nelson,

Inc., 2001). Originally published (Dallas, TX: Word Publishing, 1997), 41.

4. Isaiah 65:24 (*MSG*)

Chapter 10

"Jeeping" over Unknown Terrain

1. Janis M. Brizendine, "*Turmoil*"
2. James 5:16 (*MSG*)
3. II Corinthians 5:17 (*NIV*)
4. II Corinthians 12:9 (*NIV*)
5. Romans 3:20 (*NIV*)
6. Isaiah 40:29–31 (*NIV*)

Chapter 11

Anger, Guilt, Depression, and "Why?" Questions

1. Jessica Shaver Renshaw, Copyright © 1989, "*I Told God I Was Angry*"
2. Patsy Clairmont, *Under His Wings*. Previously published (Colorado Springs, CO: Focus on the Family Publishing, 1994), 141. Used by permission of Patsy Clairmont.
3. I John 1:9 (*God's Word*)
4. Matthew 6:14–15 (*MSG*)
5. Matthew 6:34 (*MSG*)

Chapter 12

Emotions—a Misleading and Unreliable Gauge

1. Dr. James Dobson, *When God Doesn't Make Sense* (Wheaton, IL: Tyndale House Publishers, Inc., 1993), 46.
2. Psalm 139:7–10 (*God's Word*)
3. Joyce Meyer, *Managing Your Emotions* (New York, NY: Faith Words, 2002). Previously published (New York, NY: Warner Faith, 1997), 37.
4. Ibid., 37–38.

Chapter 13

Thoughts Are Powerful

1. Shad Helmstetter, Ph.D. *What To Say When You Talk To Your Self.* Previously published (New York, NY: Pocket Books, a division of Simon & Schuster, Inc., 1982), back cover. Used by permission of Dr. Shad Helmstetter.
2. Ibid., 23. Used by permission of Dr. Shad Helmstetter.
3. Ibid., 162–163. Used by permission of Dr. Shad Helmstetter.
4. Charles R. Swindoll, *Strengthening Your Grip* (Nashville, TN: W Publishing Group, 1982), 206–07. Used by permission of Insight for Living, Plano, TX 75025.
5. Isaiah 43:18–19 (*MSG*)
6. Joel Osteen, *Your Best Life Now Journal* (New York, NY: Faith Words, 2005). Previously published (New York, NY: Warner Faith, 2005), 64.
7. Romans 12:2–3 (*MSG*)
8. Psalm 32:8 (*NLT*)
9. Proverbs 23:7 (*NKJV*)
10. Joel Osteen, *Your Best Life Now* (New York, NY: Faith Words, 2004). Previously published (New York, NY: Warner Faith, 2004), 109–110.
11. H. Norman Wright, *Experiencing Grief* (Nashville, TN: Broadman & Holman Publishers, 2004), 53.
12. Ibid., 53.
13. Psalm 18:24, 30 (*MSG*)
14. Romans 8:26–28 (*MSG*)
15. Alla Bozarth-Campbell, Ph.D., *Life Is Goodbye/Life Is Hello, 7.*

Chapter 14

Acknowledging Your Loss Is Crucial to Healing

1. Janis M. Brizendine, "*Grief*"

Chapter 15

Release: Endings and Beginnings

1. Hal Larson and Susan Larson, *Suddenly Single* (San Francisco, CA: Halo Books, 1990), 157.

Chapter 17

Remapping 101: Will You Take the Risk?

1. John E. Welshons, *Awakening from Grief,* 12.
2. Ibid., 42.

Chapter 18

Laughter—Unbelievable "Medicine"

1. Richard Williams, "Humor as a Therapeutic Recreation Intervention," *Parks & Recreation,* May 2002.
2. Article by Kevin Kelly, Editor of the *Whole Earth Review* (based on a telephone interview with Norman Cousins). *Whole Earth Review,* No. 61, Winter 1988.
3. Jan Manaway, Untitled Poem
4. Psalm 34:18 (*MSG*)

Note: Dr. Lee S. Berk quote, Dr. William F. Fry, Jr. quote, and general information about laughter's effects on the body were taken from the collection of resources cited under Sources on Laughter, Humor Therapy, and Health.

Chapter 19

Our Timing—or God's?

1. II Peter 3:8–9 (*God's Word*)
2. Isaiah 55:8 (*NLT*)
3. I Thessalonians 2:13 (*AMP*)
4. Romans 12:2 (*NLT*); Philippians 2:13 (*NLT*)

5. Nehemiah 9:19, 21 (*NIV*)
6. Matthew 9:29 (*NLT*)

Chapter 20

Learning to Embrace Solitude

1. Earl A. Grollman, *Living When a Loved One Has Died,* 91.
2. Jim Stephens quote from *Grace Notes,* Resource Ministries International. Note: Permission granted by Mr. Stephens to reprint quote.
3. Psalm 46:10 (*NLT*)

Chapter 21

Metamorphosis—from Pain to New Beginnings

1. Judy Brizendine, *"A New Song . . . of Life"*
2. James Edwards quote from *The Divine Intruder.* Note: Book is out of print. Publisher directed me to Mr. Edwards—who granted permission to reprint.
3. Hebrews 6:18–20 (*MSG*)
4. Phil Munsey, *Legacy Now* (Lake Mary, FL: Charisma House, 2007), 56.

Interactive Exercises: The Road to Healing

1. Psalm 91:15 (*NLT*)

Hope

1. Judy Brizendine, *"Signs of a New Beginning"*
2. *Things I've Learned about Grief*
3. Chelle Thompson, Copyright © 2003, *"The Ripple Effect"*
4. Unknown author, *"Your Destiny"*
5. Psalm 5:11 (*MSG*)
6. Psalm 18:20 (*MSG*)
7. Psalm 62:7–8 (*MSG*)
8. Psalm 63:8 (*MSG*)

9. Psalm 37:5 (*MSG*)
10. Psalm 91:11–12 (*MSG*)
11. Psalm 121:7–8 (*MSG*)
12. Psalm 94:17–19 (*MSG*)
13. Proverbs 13:12 (*MSG*)
14. Matthew 19:26 (*NLT*)
15. II Chronicles 20:15 (*NLT*)
16. Matthew 5:3 (*MSG*)
17. I Corinthians 2:9 (*MSG*)
18. Matthew 5:18 (*MSG*)
19. Matthew 11:28–30 (*MSG*)
20. Ephesians 3:20 (*MSG*)
21. Hebrews 11:1 (*MSG*)
22. Philippians 4:6–7 (*God's Word*)
23. Isaiah 43:10b–11 (*God's Word*)
24. 1 John 5:13–15 (*MSG*)
25. Isaiah 43:1–4 (*MSG*)
26. Psalm 23:1–6 (*MSG*)

Epilogue

1. Bernie S. Siegel, M.D., *Peace, Love, & Healing* (New York: Harper & Row, Publishers, 1989), 3.

EXTENSION OF
THE COPYRIGHT PAGE

DISCLAIMER

The purpose of this book is to help people learn about grief, and the author has made every effort to provide accurate and authoritative information about this book's subject matter; however, the book is not all-inclusive.

This book is sold with the understanding that neither the author nor the publisher are engaged in rendering medical, psychological, or other professional advice, and that the author and publisher disclaim all responsibility or any liability arising either directly or indirectly from adherence to any advice contained within, or actions taken because of information contained in this book. Its ideas and suggestions are intended to supplement, not replace, the advice of a trained medical or psychological professional. If personal assistance of any kind is required, a competent professional should be consulted.

Although the author extensively researched sources for this book, it is possible that errors, omissions, or other inconsistencies may be found. The author and publisher assume no responsibility for such errors, including accurate citation of sources. Apologies are extended for any such errors or omissions; please notify the publisher of such, and corrections will gladly be made in future editions. Any perceived slights against people or organizations are unintentional.

The author has attempted to locate the source of all material included in this edition of *STUNNED by Grief*. Grateful acknowledgment is made to individuals and publishers who have kindly granted permission for the use of their materials in this edition of *STUNNED by Grief*. If there are instances where proper credit is not given, the publisher will gladly make necessary corrections in subsequent printings.

Internet addresses printed in this book are not intended to be or imply an endorsement on the part of the publisher or the author, nor do we vouch for the content of these sites or the addresses for the life of the book. Further, the publisher does not have any control over and does not assume any responsibility for third-party websites or their content.

Names, personal descriptions, and circumstantial details in case-study narratives have been altered to protect the privacy of individuals.

SELECTED BIBLIOGRAPHY
AND RECOMMENDED READING

Arterburn, Stephen, M.Ed. *Healing Is a Choice.* Nashville, TN: Thomas Nelson, Inc., 2005.

Bozarth, Alla Renée, Ph.D. *Life Is Goodbye/Life Is Hello.* Center City, MN: Hazelden Educational Materials, 1994.

Bozarth-Campbell, Alla. *Understanding Grief.* New York, NY: Brunner-Routledge, 1992.

Caplan, Sandi and Lang, Gordon. *Grief's Courageous Journey.* Oakland, CA: New Harbinger Publications, Inc., 1995.

Clairmont, Patsy. *Under His Wings.* Colorado Springs, CO: Focus on the Family Publishing, 1994.

Cloud, Dr. Henry and Townsend, Dr. John. *How People Grow.* Grand Rapids, MI: Zondervan, 2001.

Colgrove, Melba, Ph.D., Bloomfield, Harold H., M.D., & McWilliams, Peter. *How to Survive the Loss of a Love.* Los Angeles, CA: Prelude Press, 1976, 1991.

Cornils, Stanley P. *The Mourning After—How to Manage Grief Wisely.* Saratoga, CA: R&E Publishers, 1992.

Didion, Joan. *The Year of Magical Thinking.* New York, NY: Alfred A. Knopf, a division of Random House, Inc., 2005.

Dobson, James. *When God Doesn't Make Sense.* Wheaton, IL: Tyndale House Publishers, Inc., 1993.

Grollman, Earl A. *Living When a Loved One Has Died.* Boston, MA: Beacon Press, 1995.

Helmstetter, Shad, Ph.D. *What to Say When You Talk to Your Self.* New York, NY: Pocket Books, a division of Simon & Schuster, Inc., 1982.

Hickman, Martha Whitmore. *Healing After Loss.* New York, NY: Avon Books, Inc., 1994.

James, John W. and Cherry, Frank. *The Grief Recovery Handbook.* New York, NY: Harper & Row, Publishers, 1988.

Johnson, Barbara. *Splashes of Joy in the Cesspools of Life.* Dallas, TX: Word Publishing, 1992.

Larson, Hal and Larson, Susan. *Suddenly Single.* San Francisco, CA: Halo Books, 1990.

Lucado, Max. *When God Whispers Your Name.* Nashville, TN: W Publishing Group, a division of Thomas Nelson, Inc., 1994, 1999.

Manning, Doug. *The Pain of Grief* (Continuing Care Series, Book 1). Oklahoma City, OK: In-Sight Books, Inc., 2002.

Manning, Doug. *The Reality of Grief* (Continuing Care Series, Book 2). Oklahoma City, OK: In-Sight Books, Inc., 2002.

Manning, Doug. *The Dimensions of Grief* (Continuing Care Series, Book 3). Oklahoma City, OK: In-Sight Books, Inc., 2002.

Manning, Doug. *The Journey of Grief* (Continuing Care Series, Book 4). Oklahoma City, OK: In-Sight Books, Inc., 2002.

Marr, Diane Dempsey. *The Reluctant Traveler.* Colorado Springs, CO: NavPress, 2002.

Meyer, Joyce. *Managing Your Emotions.* New York, NY: Faith Words, 2002. (Previously by Warner Faith, Time Warner Book Group, 1997).

Munsey, Phil. *Legacy Now: Why Everything about You Matters.* Lake Mary, FL: Charisma House, 2008.

Osteen, Joel. *Your Best Life Now.* New York, NY: Faith Words. (Previously by Warner Faith, 2004).

Osteen, Joel. *Your Best Life Now Journal.* New York, NY: Faith Words. (Previously by Warner Faith, 2005).

Schwiebert, Pat and DeKlyen, Chuck. *Tear Soup.* Portland, OR: Grief Watch, 1999.

Siegel, Bernie, S., M.D. *Peace, Love, & Healing.* Quill, 1998. (Previously by Harper & Row, Publishers, 1989).

Smith, Joanne and Biggs, Judy. *How to Say Goodbye.* Lynnwood, WA: Aglow Publications, 1990.

Talbot, Toby. *A Book About My Mother.* New York: Farrar, Straus and Giroux, 1980.

Warren, Rick. *The Purpose Driven Life.* Grand Rapids, MI: Zondervan, 2002.

Welshons, John E. *Awakening from Grief.* Novato, CA: New World Library. (Previously by Makawao, Maui, HI: Inner Ocean Publishing, Inc., 2003).

Westberg, Granger E. *Good Grief.* Philadelphia, PA: Fortress Press, 1962, 1971.

Wolfelt, Alan. *Understanding Grief.* New York, NY: Brunner-Routledge, an imprint of Taylor & Francis Books, Inc., 1992.

Wright, H. Norman. *Experiencing Grief.* Nashville, TN: Broadman & Holman Publishers, 2004.

Wunnenberg, Kathe. *Grieving the Loss of a Loved One.* Grand Rapids, MI: Zondervan, 2000.

SOURCES ON LAUGHTER, HUMOR THERAPY, AND HEALTH

Cousins, Norman. *Anatomy of an Illness.* New York, NY: W.W. Norton & Company, 1979.

Allwardt, Debra; Jose, Helena; Parreira, Pedro; Thorson, James A. "A factor-analytic study of the multidimensional sense of humor scale with a Portuguese sample," *North American Journal of Psychology,* (December 1, 2007).

Bennett, Howard J., M.D. "Humor in Medicine," *Southern Medical Journal* 96, no. 12 (December 2003): 1257–61.

Berk, Dr. L.S., P.H., M.P.H., and Tan, Stanley, M.D., Ph.D. "The Laughter-Immune Connection: New Discoveries," *Humor & Health Journal* 5, no. 5 (September–October 1996): 1–5.

Christie, Wanda, MNSc, RN, OCN, and Moore, Carole, BSN, RN, CEN. "The Impact of Humor on Patients with Cancer," *Clinical Journal of Oncology Nursing* 9, no. 2 (April 2005): 211–18.

Dunn, J.R., interviewing L.S. Berk, "New Discoveries in Psychoneuroimmunology," *Humor & Health Letter* 3, no. 6 (November–December 1994): 1–8.

Godfrey, Jodi R., M.S., R.D. "Toward Optimal Health: The Experts Discuss Therapeutic Humor," *Journal of Women's Health* 13, no. 5 (2004): 474–79.

Hostetler, Jep, "Humor, Spirituality, and Well-Being," *Perspectives on Science and Christian Faith* 54, no. 2 (June 2002): 108–13.

Online articles/resources/references:

Bennett, Sandy. (November 1, 2001). Irvine researcher studying the connection between laughter and health. *OC Metro Business.*

http://www.ocmetro.com/archives/ocmetro_2001/metro110101/ hot25/berk.html. [Note: online archives currently go back only to 2002]

Berk, Ron, PhD (updated 2008 by Martin, Rod, PhD, Baird, Don, PsyD, and Nozik, Bob, MD). What Everyone Should Know about Humor & Laughter. Association for Applied and Therapeutic Humor. http://www.aath.org/documents/AATH-WhatWeKnowREVISED.pdf.

Brain, Marshall. (April 1, 2000). How Laughter Works. Discovery Health. http://health.howstuffworks.com/mental-health/human-nature/other-emotions/laughter.htm.

Branigan, Lisa. Laughter and Your Health. *Ezine Articles.* http://ezinearticles.com/?Laughter-and-Your-Health&id=9451.

Carlson, Sylvia. (April 24, 2007). Stress Reduction thru Humor— How to Lighten up and Laugh Yourself Well. Suite101.com. http://relaxation-stress-reduction.suite101.com/article.cfm/stress_reduction_thru_humor.

Diggs, Tammie S. Laughter: Is It Healthy? http://hiwaay.net/~garson/laughter.htm.

Ferguson, Chad. (October 9, 2007). It's No Joke, Laughter Is Awesome Medicine. PR-Com . . . News from Origin. http://www.pr-gb-com/index.php?_option=com_content&task=view&id=28781&Itemid=9.

Fusco, S. CEC Article—Laughter, Jest for the Health of It. http://www.aquacert.org/cec42005.pdf.

Gallozzi, Chuck. Benefits of Laughter. http://www.personal-development.com/chuck/laughter.htm.

Gallozzi, Chuck. Learning to Laugh. http://www.personal-development.com/chuck/learning-to-laugh.htm.

Goldsmith, Barton. (December 17, 2007). Emotional Fitness: Some tools to help find the route to happiness. *Ventura County Star.* http://www.venturacountystar.com/news/2007/dec/17/some-tools-to-help-find-the-route-to-happiness/.

Griffin, R. Morgan. Give Your Body a Boost—With Laughter: Why, for some, laughter is the best medicine. Web MD. http://women.webmd.com/guide/give-your-body-boost-with-laughter.

How moods affect our health. (December 11, 2007). *The Independent.* http://www.independent.co.uk/life-style/health-and-wellbeing/ healthy-living/how-moods-affect-our-health-764289.html.

Humor Therapy. http://www.holistic-online.com/stress/stress_humor.htm.

Humour References (bibliography of resources). http://www.humour foundation.com.au/index.php?page=224.

The Infography about Humor Therapy (bibliography of resources). http://www.infography.com/content/915646484548.html.

Johnson, Sharon. (October 16, 2007). Laugh yourself into better health. *Mail Tribune.* http://mailtribune.com/apps/pbcs.dll/ article?AID=/20071016/LIFE/710160302.

Kay, Dr., and Max, Dr. (October 28, 2007). Integrative Way: Go ahead and laugh—it's good for you. *The Sacramento Bee.* http://www.sacbee. com/107/story/454398.html.

Koerner, Pete. The Secret to Happiness. *Ezine Articles.* http://ezinearticles. com/?The-Secret-to-Happiness&id=1055830.

Lamprecht, Melanie. (August 13, 2007). Therapeutic Humor—Value of Humor to Health Care Professionals and Patients. Suite 101. http://generalmedicine.suite101.com/article.cfm/therapeutic_humor.

Laughter as Therapy. http://www.crystalinks.com/laughter.html.

Laughter is the Best Medicine: The Health Benefits of Humor and Laughter. http://www.helpguide.org/life/humor_laughter_health.htm.

Laughter research conducted at LLUMC. (March 11, 1999). *Loma Linda University School of Medicine News.* http://www.llu.edu/pages/news/ today/mar99/sm.htm.

Laughter: The Ageless Prescription for Good Health. http://justlaughter. com/ageless_prescription.htm.

Laughter Therapy. http://www.indiadiets.com/Alternative%20Healing/ Laughter.htm.

Love, Joe. Developing Your Sense of Humor. *Ezine Articles.* http://ezinearticles.com/?Developing-Your-Sense-Of-Humor&id=181073.

Reynolds, Joyce K. The Many Benefits of Laughter. *CoachTALK.* Volume III, May 2002. http://www.jkr.net/newsletter/coachtalk2002-05.htm.

Schiller, Pam, Ph.D. A Case for Laughing, Giggling, and Having Fun. Kimbo Educational. https://www.kimboed.com/index.asp?PageAction=Custom&ID=22.

Scott, Elizabeth, M.S. The Stress Management and Health Benefits of Laughter. (October 7, 2009). About.com: Stress Management. http://stress.about.com/od/stresshealth/a/laughter.htm.

Therapeutic Benefits of Laughter. Holistic online. http://www.holisticon-line.com/Humor_Therapy/humor_therapy_benefits.htm.

Uffindell, Sarah. Laugh and be healthy. *College and University DIALOGUE, An International Journal of Faith, Thought, and Action.* http://dialogue.adventist.org/articles10_3_uffindell_e.htm.

The Use of Humor & Laughter in Therapy. LCSWethics. http://lcswethics.com/texts/humor-and-laughter-therapy.html.

Warren, Rick. (July 13, 2007). Learn to Laugh. *Christian Post.* http://www.christianpost.com/article/20070713/learn-to-laugh/index.htm.

Why a good laugh inspires a better life. *The Standard* (December 20, 2007). http://216.180.252.4/archives/index.php?mnu=details&id=1143979151&catid=318.

Wojciechowski, Michael. Tickling the Funny Bone—The Use and Benefits of Humor in Health Care. American Physical Therapy Association (APTA). http://www.apta.org/AM/Template.cfm?Section=Home&TEMPLATE=/CM/HTMLDisplay.cfm&CONTENTID=45278.

Wooten, Patty. Laughter as Therapy for Patient and Caregiver. http://www.jesthealth.com/ch_pulm.html.

INDEX

.

HOW TO
CONTACT THE AUTHOR

To reach Judy Brizendine and find additional resources,
please visit the website:
www.stunnedbygrief.com

Or write to:
Judy Brizendine
c/o BennettKnepp Publishing
P.O. Box 296
Lake Forest, CA 92609-0296

If you would like to tell me about your experience or
give feedback on the book or journal, I'd love to hear from you.
My email address is:
jbriz@stunnedbygrief.com

Additional copies of *STUNNED by Grief* and the
STUNNED by Grief Journal
can be ordered online:
www.stunnedbygrief.com

BennettKnepp
PUBLISHING

Lake Forest, CA

BennettKnepp is dedicated to producing books that effect positive change in the lives of individuals and the world. Our goal is to engage, inform, delight, and transform people through the written word.

We value our readers' opinions and encourage your feedback. To make comments about our books or offer suggestions, please write to us.

BennettKnepp Publishing
P.O. Box 296
Lake Forest, CA 92609-0296

www.bennettknepp.com

This book is available at special quantity discounts for bulk purchases by businesses, organizations, churches, and special-interest groups. Customized books, booklets, or excerpts can be created to fit specific needs. For information, please contact the publisher.